# DIRECTO AL GRANO

## A complete reference manual for Spanish Grammar

*Priscilla Gac-Artigas*

Monmouth University


*Gustavo Gac-Artigas*

Prentice Hall, Upper Saddle River, NJ 07458

**Library of Congress Cataloging-in-Publication Data**

Gac-Artigas, Priscilla.
        Directo al grano: a complete reference manual for Spanish grammar / Priscilla and Gustavo
Gac-Artigas.
        p. cm.
        ISBN 0-13-084801-8
1. Spanish language -- Grammar -- Handbooks, manuals, etc.
I. Gac-Artigas, Gustavo, 10/27/99
PC41121.G83  1999
465--dc21
                                99-045749

*To Melina and Alejandro Gac-Artigas,*
*who granted us part of the precious time*
*of their childhood to complete this book.*

Editor in Chief: Rosemary Bradley
Development Editor: Mariam Pérez-Roch Rohlfing
Executive Managing Editor: Ann Marie McCarthy
Project Manager: Elizabeth Dice
Interior Design: Hispanex, Inc.
Cover Design: Bruce Kenselaar
Buyer: Tricia Kenny
Executive Marketing Manager: Ilse Wolfe

This book was set in 11/13 point Sabon by Hispanex, Inc.,
and was printed and bound by Courier Companies, Inc.
The cover was printed by Phoenix Color Corp.

©2000 by Prentice-Hall, Inc.
Upper Saddle River, New Jersey 07458

First and second editions previously
published by To the Point Books.

Printed in the United States of America
10 9 8 7 6 5 4 3 2 1

ISBN   0-13-084801-8

PRENTICE-HALL INTERNATIONAL (UK) LIMITED, *London*
PRENTICE-HALL OF AUSTRALIA PTY. LIMITED, *Sydney*
PRENTICE-HALL CANADA INC., *Toronto*
PRENTICE-HALL HISPANOAMERICANA, S.A., *Mexico*
PRENTICE-HALL OF INDIA PRIVATE LIMITED, *New Delhi*
PRENTICE-HALL OF JAPAN, INC., *Tokyo*
PEARSON EDUCATION ASIA PTE. LTD., *Singapore*
EDITORA PRENTICE-HALL DO BRASIL, LTDA., *Rio de Janeiro*

# CONTENTS

# PREFACE

**Directo al Grano** is an indispensable, complete, student-friendly and self-teaching grammar reference book for beginners as well as advanced students of Spanish.

Because it is succinct, clear and easy to consult, **Directo al Grano** always goes to the point, which makes it excellent for reference. The book solves, at a glance, any doubt about the use of Spanish. Concise, accurate and informative descriptions cover all the complexity of specific grammatical points, thus saving a large amount of time for students who are writing papers or reviewing for tests.

The mastery of a language is measured by one's ability to express oneself in a coherent way, with a vocabulary that goes beyond the minimum required for survival or grammatical accuracy. The conceptual economy of the charts and formulas included in **Directo al Grano** assures mastery in the clearest, fastest and most effortless way possible.

Beyond the classroom, **Directo al Grano** provides a lifelong reference guide for anybody eager to learn the Spanish language.

# ACKNOWLEDGMENTS

We would like to thank

Rosemary Bradley, Editor in Chief, and Mariam Rohlfing, our Editor. Thanks for your wise suggestions and your understanding of our purpose; for your smiles and graciousness. It has been a pleasure working with both of you.

We would also like to thank our colleagues at different universities throughout the country for helping us revise the first version of **Directo al Grano**. Their comments and suggestions were most valuable to our work in this text. Among these colleagues we would like to thank: Luisa C. Pérez, *Emporia State University*; Hildegart Hoquee, *San Jacinto College*; and Cecilia Ryan, *McNeese State University*.

Finally, we want to thank the technical team at Prentice Hall involved in the production of **Directo al Grano**. Thank you to Ann Marie McCarthy, Executive Managing Editor.

# CHAPTER 1

## *Articles*

**ARTICLES** are words used before a noun to limit or give definiteness to its application. They signal the presence of a noun.

✔ Articles are classified as definite or indefinite.

✔ Articles are either masculine or feminine, singular or plural, according to the gender and number of the noun with which they are used.

✔ In Spanish the names of things as well as living beings have gender.

**1-1  Definite articles** *refer to specific members of a group or class.*

✔ Definite articles agree in gender and number with the noun they modify.

|           | singular | plural |
|-----------|----------|--------|
| masculine | el       | los    |
| feminine  | la*      | las    |

*in front of a feminine noun starting with stressed **a** or **ha,** use **el** instead of **la.** See Nouns p. 9.

### Definite Articles

✔ Definite articles are equivalent to **the.**

### 1-1a  Definite articles in front of nouns: uses and omissions

✔ Definite articles are used with titles, except before **Don** and **Doña,** when talking about someone, i.e., indirect address.

Es **el** doctor González.
*It is Doctor González.*

¿Viste a **la** señorita Pérez?
*Did you see Miss Pérez?*

¿Viste a don Francisco?
*Did you see Don Francisco?*

✔ Use definite articles when the proper or last names appear in plural form.

En mi clase predominan **las** Marías.
*In my class Marías predominate.*

Ayer fui a visitar a **los** Soto.
*Yesterday I went to visit the Sotos.*

✔ When proper names are used as metaphors, use a definite article.

En esta conferencia de escritores no abundan **los** Cervantes, en cambio **los** Sanchos pululan.
*In this conference of writers, Cervantes are absent, but Sanchos swarm.*

✔ Use a definite article after the preposition **de** when the complement of the preposition is specific.

Es una antología de **la** narrativa de Gustavo Gac-Artigas.
*It is an anthology of Gustavo Gac-Artigas' fiction.*

✔ Definite articles appear before a noun used in a general sense as representative of its class or type, or as a stereotype.

Los brasileños son muy buenos futbolistas.
*Brazilians are very good soccer players.*

✔ Use a definite article before each noun in a series.

El departamento es un desastre. No funcionan ni **las** luces, ni **el** aire acondicionado, ni **la** cocina.
*The apartment is a mess; neither the lights, the air conditioning, nor the kitchen is working.*

✔ Definite articles are used with parts of the body, personal belongings and articles of clothing, when it is clear who the possessor is.

Melina se lava **el** pelo.　　　　　Alejandro se puso **la** chaqueta.
*Melina washes her hair.*　　　　　*Alejandro put on his jacket.*

✔ If the noun is modified, the possessive adjective is used as it is in English.

Melina se lava su hermoso pelo.
*Melina washes her beautiful hair.*

## Omissions

✘ Definite articles are omitted when addressing someone directly.

Hasta mañana, doctor González.
*See you tomorrow, Doctor González.*

✘ Omit definite articles in front of proper names.

Antonio, Ignacio y Sara fueron al cine.
*Antonio, Ignacio, and Sara went to the movies.*

## It is not correct to say

El Antonio, el Ignacio y la Sara...
*The Antonio, the Ignacio, and the Sara.*

✘ Definite articles are omitted when the complement of the preposition indicates a general characteristic.

Es una antología de cuentos.
*It is an anthology of short stories.*

✘ Definite articles are omitted when the reference is to part of a general class or type.

En mi clase hay chilenos que hablan inglés.
*There are Chileans in my class who speak English.*

✘ Definite articles are omitted before an abstract noun used to express an indefinite quantity.

Siente amor por la lectura.
*He/She loves reading.*

✘ Definite articles are omitted before a concrete noun referring to a quantity that cannot be counted, or to a part of a whole.

Usé harina, huevos, sal y leche para hacer la torta.
*I used flour, eggs, salt and milk to make the cake.*

Anoche comí pollo y ensalada.
*Last night I ate chicken and salad.*

✘ Definite articles are omitted with names of languages or fields of study, after the prepositions **de** and **en**, and after the verbs **hablar**\*, **escribir**\*, **leer**\* (\*unmodified), **estudiar**, and **aprender**.

¿Hablas español?
Sí, hablo español. Gracias a mi profesora de español hablo **el** español correctamente.
*Do you speak Spanish?*
*Yes, I speak Spanish. Thanks to my Spanish professor, I speak Spanish correctly.*

### 1-1b  Definite articles in front of days, dates, time, seasons, prices, and rates: uses and omissions

✔ Definite articles are used with the days of the week, except after the verb **ser**. In English this would be translated as **on**.

Siempre vamos a bailar **los** viernes.
*We always go dancing on Fridays.*

✔ Definite articles are used with dates and seasons

El examen final será **el** 21 de junio.          Mi estación favorita es **la** primavera.
*The final exam will be June 21.*              *Spring is my favorite season.*

✘ Definite articles are omitted when the day of the week comes after **ser**.

Hoy es miércoles.
*Today is Wednesday.*

✘ Definite articles can be omitted after the preposition **en.**

Prefiero viajar en verano.
*I prefer to travel during the summer.*

✔ Definite articles come before the adjectives **pasado** and **próximo,** when they appear in front of the noun.

Luis se gradúa **el** próximo año.            Luis se gradúa **el** año próximo.
*Luis will graduate next year.*              *Luis will graduate next year.*

✔ Definite articles are used with rates and prices.

¿Cuánto cuestan las sandías?            Dos pesos **la** libra.
*How much are the watermelons?*          *Two pesos a pound.*

✔ **La** or **las** is used with cardinal numbers to tell time.

Es **la** una y a **las** cinco en punto asesinarán al poeta.
*It is one o'clock, and the poet will be murdered at five.*

✔ The definite article **el** is used in front of infinitives that function as nouns.

**El** viajar es enriquecedor.            **El** no fumar es bueno para la salud.
*Traveling is enriching.*                *It's good for your health not to smoke.*

## 1-1c   Contractions: del / al

✔ The definite article **el** contracts after the prepositions **de** and **a.**

de el → **del**                          a el → **al**

Éste es el libro **del** (de el) profesor.       ¿Vamos **al** (a el) cine?
*This is the teacher's book.*             *Are we going to the movies?*

✘ Do not make the contraction if the article is part of a proper name.

Mañana iremos **a El** Escorial.            Es una foto **de El** Escorial.
*Tomorrow we will go to The Escorial.*      *It is a picture of The Escorial.*

✘ Do not contract with the subject pronoun **él.**

¿Ese libro es **de él?**
*Is that book his?*

**1-2 Indefinite articles** *refer to any unspecified member of a general group or class.*

✔ The singular forms of indefinite articles correspond to **a** and **an,** and the plural forms to **some** or **a few** (restrictive quantity). In some cases indefinite articles express **about** or **around** (approximative quantity).

✔ Indefinite articles agree in number and gender with the noun they modify.

|  | singular | plural |
|---|---|---|
| masculine | un *a/an* | unos *some/a few/about* |
| feminine | una* *a/an* | unas *some/a few/about* |

## 1-2a  Indefinite articles: uses and omissions

*in front of a feminine noun starting with stressed **a** or **ha**, use **un** instead of **una**. See Nouns p. 9.

✔ Before a singular masculine noun, **un** is used.

**un** hombre *a man*        **un** libro *a book*        **un** árbol *a tree*

**Un** día lunes triste hasta el infinito, pero aun más triste al ser **un** frío lunes de invierno…
*A sad Monday, infinitely sad, and because it was a cold winter Monday it was even sadder…*

✔ Note that **uno**, meaning *one*, is shortened to **un** in front of a masculine noun.

Usé **un** tomate y dos cebollas para hacer la ensalada.
*I used a tomato and two onions to prepare the salad.*

✔ Before a singular feminine noun, **una** is used.

**una** mujer *a woman*            **una** casa *a house*            **una** manzana *an apple*

✔ Use **un** instead of **una** when the feminine noun starts with a stressed **a** or **ha**.

Había **un** águila en el nido.
*There was an eagle in the nest.*

✔ Approximation is frequently translated by **unos** or **unas**.

Tenía **unos** ochenta años cuando murió.
*He/She was about eighty years old when he/she died.*

✔ The indefinite articles are repeated before each noun in a series.

Soy rico, tengo **una** flor, **una** nube y **un** unicornio.
*I am rich; I own a flower, a cloud, and a unicorn.*

En sueños devoré **una** empanada, **un** plato de cazuela, **un** asado y, de postre, **una** manzana de esas que crecen en el sur de Chile.
*In my dreams, I devoured an empanada, a casserole, a plate of barbecue, and for dessert, one of those apples that grow in the south of Chile.*

✗ Indefinite articles are never used before **medio/media** and **otro/otra,** and frequently omitted before **cierto.**

> Quiero media libra de jamón.
> *I want half a pound of ham.*

> La vida es sueño, como dijo cierto dramaturgo.
> *Life is a dream, as a certain playwright said.*

> María compró otro par de zapatos.
> *María bought another pair of shoes.*

✗ After the verb **ser,** indefinite articles are not used with words designating profession, political belief, religion or nationality, unless the noun is modified or stressed.

> Es escritor.
> *He is a writer.*

> Cierto, es **un** escritor genial.
> *It is true, he is a brilliant writer.*

✗ Indefinite articles are omitted after the preposition **de** in negative expressions with **tener.** They are generally omitted after the preposition **sin.**

> Mariana trabaja **de** cocinera.
> *Mariana works as a cook.*

> Juan vino **sin** chaqueta.
> *Juan came without his jacket.*

> ¡Qué afortunados! Ellos **no tienen** televisor.
> *How lucky they are! They do not own a television set.*

✗ Indefinite articles are frequently omitted with nouns in general, when the idea of quantity is not emphasized.

> ¿Tienes tiempo?
> *Do you have time?*

> ¿Hay libros de García Márquez en la biblioteca?
> *Are there any books by García Márquez at the library?*

✗ Indefinite articles are also omitted in exclamations using **¡qué! + noun.**

> ¡Qué niño tan inteligente!
> *What an intelligent boy!*

# CHAPTER 2

## Nouns

A **NOUN** is a word used to identify the subject of discourse. Nouns name persons, places, objects, or ideas.

### 2-1  Gender of nouns

2-1a  **Masculine nouns:** nouns referring to beings of the male sex are masculine.

Nouns ending in the letters   -l  -o  -n  -e  -r   are usually masculine.

Common exceptions:

| | | | |
|---|---|---|---|
| **la** cal<br>*lime* | **la** calle<br>*street* | **la** cárcel<br>*jail* | **la** catedral<br>*cathedral* |
| **la** clase<br>*class* | **la** fiebre<br>*fever* | **la** flor<br>*flower* | **la** foto<br>*picture* |
| **la** gente<br>*people* | **la** imagen<br>*image* | **la** leche<br>*milk* | **la** llave<br>*key* |
| **la** mano<br>*hand* | **la** miel<br>*honey* | **la** moral<br>*morale* | **la** moto<br>*motorcycle* |
| **la** muerte<br>*death* | **la** noche<br>*night* | **la** nube<br>*cloud* | **la** parte<br>*part* |
| **la** peste<br>*plague* | **la** piel<br>*skin* | **la** razón<br>*reason* | **la** sal<br>*salt* |
| **la** sartén<br>*frying pan* | **la** señal<br>*sign, signal* | **la** suerte<br>*chance* | **la** tarde<br>*afternoon* |

**2-1b Feminine nouns:** nouns referring to beings of the female sex are feminine.

Nouns with the following endings are usually feminine.

| -a | -ad | -d | -ción | -sión |
|-----|-------|-----|-------|-------|
| -ud | -umbre | -ie | -is | -z |

| | | | |
|---|---|---|---|
| **la** amistad *friendship* | **la** ciudad *city* | **la** costumbre *habit* | **la** crisis *crisis* |
| **la** faz *face* | **la** juventud *youth* | **la** legumbre *vegetable* | **la** muchedumbre *crowd* |
| **la** nación *nation* | **la** novela *novel* | **la** pasión *passion* | **la** paz *peace* |
| **la** raíz *root* | **la** sed *thirst* | **la** serie *serie* | **la** superficie *surface* |
| **la** televisión *tv* | **la** tesis *thesis* | **la** tez *complexion* | **la** vejez *old age* |

**Common exceptions: el análisis** *analysis,* **el día** *day,* **el lápiz** *pencil,* **el maíz** *corn,* **el sofá** *sofa,* and nouns of Greek origin ending in **-ma, -pa,** and, **-ta,** such as those that follow.

| | | |
|---|---|---|
| **el** drama *drama* | **el** mapa *map* | **el** poema *poem* |
| **el** poeta *poet* | **el** planeta *planet* | **el** programa *program* |
| **el** problema *problem* | **el** sistema *system* | **el** tema *theme, topic* |

✔ Feminine nouns beginning with stressed **a** or **ha** cannot directly follow **la** or **una; el** or **un** is used instead.

| | | | |
|---|---|---|---|
| **el** agua *water* | **un** águila *eagle* | **el** ala *wing* | **el** alma *soul* |
| **el** ama de casa *housewife* | **el** área *area* | **el** arma *weapon* | **un** aula *classroom* |
| **el** ave *bird* | **un** hacha *ax* | **el** hada *fairy* | **el** hambre *hunger* |

*but* the feminine articles are always used in the plural.

**las** águilas     **las** alas     **las** aulas     **las** hachas

✔ When an adjective intervenes between the article and the noun, the feminine article is always used.

**una** buena **hacha**
*a great ax*

Juana es **una** perfecta **ama** de casa.
*Juana is a perfect housewife.*

✔ When the noun begins with an unstressed **a** or **ha,** use the feminine article.

| **la** avenida | **la** amapola | **la** aspirina |
| *avenue* | *poppy* | *aspirin* |
| **la** aristocracia | **la** arena | **la** harina |
| *aristocracy* | *sand* | *flour* |

✔ Names of letters are feminine; names of numbers are masculine.

**la** eme     **la** o     **el** uno     **el** dos

✔ Names of the days of the week, languages, mountains*, oceans, and rivers are masculine.

**el** martes     **el** español     **los** Alpes     **el** Atlántico     **el** Sena

*with the exception of geographic nouns preceded by **Sierra** or **Cordillera.**

**La** Sierra Nevada
**La** Cordillera de Los Andes

✔ Most nouns ending in -**e** or -**ista** that refer to people, can be masculine or feminine. Context helps to determine whether the words refer to a male or a female.

| **el** artista | **la** artista | *artist* |
| **el** estudiante | **la** estudiante | *student* |
| **el** cantante | **la** cantante | *singer* |
| **el** turista | **la** turista | *tourist* |
| **el** agente | **la** agente | *agent* |
| **el** guía | **la** guía | *guide* |

✔ Some nouns can be masculine or feminine depending on their meaning. The noun itself does not change its spelling.

| | |
|---|---|
| **el** capital | **la** capital |
| *capital (money)* | *capital (city)* |
| **el** cura | **la** cura |
| *priest* | *cure* |
| **el** corte | **la** corte |
| *cut* | *court* |
| **el** frente | **la** frente |
| *front* | *forehead* |
| **el** mañana | **la** mañana |
| *the future* | *morning* |
| **el** orden | **la** orden |
| *order (tidiness)* | *command* |
| **el** papa | **la** papa |
| *pope* | *potato* |
| **el** pez | **la** pez |
| *fish* | *tar* |

✔ The following nouns change meaning if the gender changes. Notice that the ending of the noun changes too, unlike the nouns shown above.

| | |
|---|---|
| el bando | la banda |
| *faction* | *band* |
| el derecho | la derecha |
| *right, law* | *right (direction)* |
| el fondo | la fonda |
| *bottom* | *inn* |
| el lomo | la loma |
| *back of an animal* | *hill* |
| el punto | la punta |
| *dot, period, stitch* | *point, tip* |
| el puerto | la puerta |
| *port* | *door* |

✔ Some common nouns have a completely different form in the feminine.

| | |
|---|---|
| un caballero | una dama |
| *gentleman* | *lady* |
| un hombre | una mujer |
| *man* | *woman* |
| un rey | una reina |
| *king* | *queen* |
| el padre | la madre |
| *father* | *mother* |
| el yerno | la nuera |
| *son-in-law* | *daughter-in-law* |
| un macho | una hembra |
| *male* | *female* |
| un gallo | una gallina |
| *rooster* | *hen* |
| un caballo | una yegua |
| *horse* | *mare* |

## 2-2  Plural of nouns

✔ Nouns that end in a **vowel** form the plural by adding **-s.**

la casa → las casas

el estudiante → los estudiantes

✔ Nouns ending in a **consonant, -í,** or **-ú,** form the plural by adding **-es.**

| el profesor | → los profesores | *professors* |
|---|---|---|
| el rey | → los reyes | *kings* |
| el maní | → los maníes | *peanuts* |
| el tabú | → los tabúes | *taboos* |

✗ *but* nouns ending in unstressed **-es** or **-is** do not change when they become plural.

el lunes → los lunes

el análisis → los análisis

✔ To form the plural of nouns ending in **z**, change **-z** to **-c** and add **-es**.

**z → c + es = ces**

el lápiz → los lápi**ces**    *pencil(s)*

el pez   → los pe**ces**    *fish*

✔ The plural of nouns ending in **á, é, í, ó, ú, + n,** or **s** is formed by dropping the written accent mark and adding **-es**.

botín    → botines    *plunder* or *loot*

compás → compases    *compass(es)*

lección → lecciones    *lesson(s)*

| CHART 1 | NOUNS SINGULAR / PLURAL | |
|---|---|---|
| a/e/i/o/u → + s<br>í,ú          → + es | consonant → + es<br>es = es  is = is | z → c + es<br>á/é/í/ó/ú + n/s → a/e/i/o/u + n/s + es |

Compound nouns form plurals based on the following rules.

| CHART 2 | PLURALS OF COMPOUND NOUNS |
|---|---|
| noun + noun juxtaposed<br>la telaraña  *spiderweb* | second noun becomes plural<br>las telarañas |
| adjective + noun<br>el altoparlante  *loudspeaker* | noun becomes plural<br>los altoparlantes |
| invariable word + noun<br>el superhombre  *superman* | noun becomes plural<br>los superhombres |
| noun + noun predicate<br>el coche cama  *railroad sleeping car* | first noun becomes plural<br>los coches cama |
| verb + noun object<br>el parasol  *parasol* | noun becomes plural<br>los parasoles |

# CHAPTER 3

## *Adjectives*

**ADJECTIVES** are modifiers that qualify, limit the meaning, or make a noun or pronoun more definite.

✔ Adjectives are classified as descriptive, numerical, possessive (stressed and unstressed), demonstrative, quantitative, and indefinite.

| CHART 3 | PLACEMENT OF ADJECTIVES | |

| PRECEDE | NOUN | FOLLOW |
| --- | --- | --- |
| Numerical | N | Descriptive |
| Descriptive: when used for emphasis or as a poetic device. | O | |
| Possessive unstressed | | Possessive stressed |
| Demonstrative | U | |
| Quantitative | | |
| Indefinite | N | |

## 3-1 Descriptive adjectives (*calificativos*) *express a quality of the noun.*

✔ Descriptive adjectives usually follow the noun they qualify, and must agree in gender and number with it.

Las casas **blancas** son hermosas.
*White houses are beautiful.*

✔ When used for emphasis or as a poetic device, descriptive adjectives can precede the noun.

La **blanca** lana con que tejo mis sueños.
*The white wool with which I weave my dreams.*

✔ The adjectives **mejor** and **peor** are placed in front of the noun.

Teresa es mi **mejor** amiga.
*Teresa is my best friend.*

Es el **peor** cuento que he leído.
*It is the worst short story I have ever read.*

### 3-1a Gender: feminine/masculine

✔ Adjectives ending in -**o**/-**os** change to -**a**/-**as** to agree with feminine nouns.

El hombre es alt**o**.
*The man is tall.*

La mujer es alt**a**.
*The woman is tall.*

|          | masculine | feminine |
|----------|-----------|----------|
| **singular** | -o        | -a       |
| **plural**   | -os       | -as      |

✔ Adjectives whose singular masculine form ends in -**a** do not change.

| hipócrit**a** | idiot**a** | entusiast**a** |
|-----------|--------|-------------|
| *hypocrite* | *idiot* | *enthusiastic* |

✔ Adjectives ending in -**e** or -**ista** have the same masculine and feminine forms.

| amable | caliente | optim**ista** |
|--------|----------|-----------|
| *kind* | *hot* | *optimistic* |

| grande | inteligente | pesim**ista** |
|--------|-------------|-----------|
| *big, large* | *intelligent* | *pessimistic* |

| interesante | pedante | masoqu**ista** |
|-------------|---------|-------------|
| *interesting* | *pedantic* | *masochistic* |

✔ If the adjective ends in a consonant, generally the same form serves for both masculine and feminine singular.

| actual | capaz | difícil | fácil | principal |
|--------|-------|---------|-------|-----------|
| *present* | *capable* | *difficult* | *easy* | *principal* |

| joven | mayor | menor | superior | universal |
|-------|-------|-------|----------|-----------|
| *young* | *older* | *younger* | *superior* | *universal* |

Exceptions are adjectives ending in -**dor**, -**ín**, -**ón**, or -**án,** and adjectives of nationality that add an **a** after the consonant.

| habla**dor**  | → habla**dora**  | *talkative* |
|-----------|------------|-----------|
| parlanch**ín** | → parlanch**ina** | *chatty* |
| juguet**ón**  | → juguet**ona**  | *playful* |
| holgaz**án**  | → holgaz**ana**  | *lazy* |
| español   | → española  | *Spanish* |

## 3-1b  Plural of adjectives

| | | |
|---|---|---|
| **CHART 4** | **ADJECTIVES: SINGULAR → PLURAL** | |

| vowel **+ -s** | consonant **+ -es** | **-z → –c + -es** |
|---|---|---|

✔ Adjectives ending in a vowel form their plural by adding **-s**.

bonito → bonitos   *pretty*

✔ Adjectives ending in a consonant form their plural by adding **-es**.

azul → azules   *blue*          hablador → habladores   *talkative*

✔ Adjectives ending in **-z** form their plural by changing **-z** to **-c** and adding **-es**.

z → c + es = ces
feliz → feli**ces**   *happy*

✔ An adjective that modifies a masculine and a feminine noun at the same time uses the masculine plural form.

Compré un suéter y una falda **hermosos**.
*I bought a beautiful sweater and skirt.*

## 3-1c  Shortening adjectives

✔ Before a masculine singular noun, the adjectives **bueno, malo, alguno, ninguno, primero,** and **tercero** drop the final **-o**.

Es un **buen** amigo pero un **mal** bailarín.          ¿Tienes **algún** amigo español?
*He is a great friend, but a bad dancer.*          *Do you have a Spanish friend?*

Mi oficina está en el **primer** piso.          No, no tengo **ningún** amigo español.
*My office is on the first floor.*          *No, I don't have a single Spanish friend.*

✔ Before an adjective or adverb, **tanto** and **cuanto** drop the final **-to,** and **reciente** drops the final **-te**.

tanto → tan          cuanto → cuan          reciente → recién

No sabes **cuán** importante eres en mi vida.
*You don't know how important you are in my life.*

Llegué **tan** tarde que no pude ver la película.
*I arrived so late that I was unable to see the movie.*

✔ **Grande** becomes **gran** before a singular noun of either gender.

Atlanta es una **gran** ciudad.
*Atlanta is a great city.*

Simón Bolívar fue un **gran** hombre.
*Simón Bolívar was a great man.*

✔ **Ciento** becomes **cien**, and **cualquiera** becomes **cualquier**, before a noun of either gender.

Leí **cien** libros.
*I read a hundred books.*

Me gusta **cualquier** comida.
*I like any kind of food.*

Trabajé **cien** horas.
*I worked a hundred hours.*

## 3-1d   Change of meaning

✔ Some adjectives change their meaning depending on whether they precede (subjective use) or follow (objective use) the noun.

- **antiguo(a)/antiguos(as)** before a noun means *former*; after a noun it means *ancient*.

  Es el **antiguo** director de la compañía.
  *He is the company's former director.*

  Es una compañía **antigua**.
  *It is an ancient company.*

- **cierto(a)/ciertos(as)** before a noun means *some*; after a noun, it means *definite*.

  **cierta** idea
  *some, a certain idea*

  una idea **cierta**
  *a true or definite idea*

- **diferente(s)** before a noun means *various*; after a noun, it means *different*.

  Consulté **diferentes** libros.
  *I consulted various books.*

  Consulté libros **diferentes**.
  *I consulted different books.*

- **grande(s)** before a noun means *great*; after a noun, it means *big*.

  ¿Es un libro **grande**?
  *Is it a big book?*

  No, pero es un **gran** libro.
  *No, but it is a great book.*

- **mismo(a)/mismos(as)** before a noun means *same*; after a noun, it means *himself/herself/themselves*.

  Es la **misma** historia.
  *It is the same old story.*

  Me lo dijo él **mismo**.
  *He told me about it himself.*

- **nuevo(a)/nuevos(as)** before a noun usually means *another*; after a noun, it means *brand new*.

  Éste es un **nuevo** libro.
  *This is another book.*

  Éste es un libro **nuevo**.
  *This is a new book.*

- **pobre(s)** before a noun means *unfortunate*; after a noun, it means *poor*.

  Es un poeta **pobre**.
  *He is an impoverished poet.*

  Es un **pobre** poeta.
  *He is an unfortunate poet.*

- **único(a)/únicos(as)** before a noun means *only;* after a noun, it means *unique.*
  exception: **hijo(a) único(a)** *only child*

  Es el **único** alumno de italiano en la sala.
  *He is the only student of Italian in the class.*

  Es un alumno **único.**
  *He is a unique student.*

- **viejo(a)/viejos(as)** before a noun means *old* (longtime); after a noun, it means *old* (elderly).

  Sempronio es un **viejo** amigo.          Tiene un amigo **viejo.**
  *Sempronio is an old (longtime) friend.*   *He/She has an old friend. (elderly)*

### 3-1e  Adjective → Adverb

✔ Adding the suffix **-mente** (*-ly*) to the feminine singular form changes the adjective into an adverb.

| | | |
|---|---|---|
| rápida | → rápida**mente** | *quickly* |
| diaria | → diaria**mente** | *daily* |
| difícil | → difícil**mente** | *with difficulty* |
| especial | → especial**mente** | *specially, especially* |
| fácil | → fácil**mente** | *easily* |

✔ When two or more adverbs modify the same word, the suffix **-mente** is only added to the last one.

Some Common Spanish Suffixes

**Adjectives:** -ante    -ble    -ivo    -ísimo    -oso
  amor**oso** *lovely*       am**ante** *lover*       ama**ble** *kind*

**Adverbs:**    -mente
  directa**mente** *directly*       veloz**mente**    *quickly*

**Verbs:**      -ar          -er          -ir
  cant**ar** *to sing*       com**er** *to eat*       dorm**ir** *to sleep*

**Nouns:**    -ancia    -ción    -ad    -ismo    -ista
  capital**ismo** *capitalism*       capital**ista** *capitalist*

**3-2  Numerical adjectives** *express number and order. They are classified as cardinal or ordinal. They precede the noun.*

3-2a  **Cardinal numbers used as adjectives** express number and are invariable, with the exception of **uno,** which agrees in gender and number with the noun. Numbers ending in **uno** or **ciento** agree only in gender.

**Un(a)**        **dos**      **tres**      **cuatro**      **cinco**

Tiene **cuatro** novelas y **veintiuna** obras de teatro publicadas.
*He/She has four novels and twenty-one plays published.*

### 3-2b Ordinal numbers used as adjectives express order.

| | | | | |
|---|---|---|---|---|
| primero | segundo | tercero | cuarto | quinto |
| *first* | *second* | *third* | *fourth* | *fifth* |
| sexto | séptimo | octavo | noveno | décimo |
| *sixth* | *seventh* | *eighth* | *ninth* | *tenth* |

## 3-3 Possessive adjectives *are modifiers used to denote possession.*

### 3-3a Unstressed possessive adjectives

✔ Unstressed possessive adjectives always precede the noun they modify.

| | singular | plural |
|---|---|---|
| *my* | mi | mis |
| *your** | tu | tus |
| *his/her/its/your* | su | sus |
| *our* | nuestro(a) | nuestros(as) |
| *your*** | vuestro(a) | vuestros(as) |
| *their/your* | su | sus |

*informal, singular
**informal, plural

Olvidé **mis** lentes en **tu** auto.
*I forgot my glasses in your car.*

**Su** novio la invitó al cine.
*Her boyfriend invited her to the movies.*

**Nuestros** padres vienen a la graduación.
*Our parents are coming to our graduation.*

✔ Unstressed possessive adjectives agree in number with the person, place or thing possessed.

Me gusta **mi** clase de español.
*I like my Spanish class.*

Tú trajiste **tus** libros y yo traje **mis** cuadernos.
*You brought your books and I brought my notebooks.*

✔ **Nuestro** and **vuestro** also agree in gender with the thing possessed, not with the possessor.

**Nuestra** casa es grande.
*Our house is big.*

**Vuestros** hijos son muy talentosos.
*Your children are very talented.*

✔ Unstressed possessive adjectives are repeated before each noun in a series.

**Mi** padre, **mi** hermana y **mi** tío vinieron a visitarnos.
*My father, my mother, and my uncle came to visit us.*

✔ The context in which **su/sus** is used can often clarify who the possessor is. If any ambiguity results from the use of **su/sus,** you can add a prepositional phrase: de + (**él, ella, usted, ustedes, ellos** or **ellas**) to indicate the owner or possessor.

| su/sus | | |
|---|---|---|
| | de usted | *your* |
| | de él | *his* |
| | de ella | *her* |
| | de ustedes | *your* |
| | de ellos | *their* |
| | de ellas | *their* |

**Su** auto es el azul.
*Your/His/Her/Their car is the blue one.*

El auto de él es el azul.
*His car is the blue one.*

El auto de ellos es el azul.
*Their car is the blue one.*

El auto de usted/de ustedes es el azul.
*Your car is the blue one.*

El auto de ella es el azul.
*Her car is the blue one.*

## 3–3b Stressed possessive adjectives

| singular | plural | |
|---|---|---|
| mío(a) | míos(as) | *of mine* |
| tuyo(a | tuyos(as) | *of yours (informal, singular)* |
| suyo(a) | suyos(as) | *of his/hers/its/theirs/of yours (formal)* |
| nuestro(a) | nuestros(as) | *of ours* |
| vuestro(a) | vuestros(as) | *of yours (informal, plural)* |

✔ Stressed possessive adjectives are used for emphasis.

✔ Stressed possessive adjectives always follow the noun they modify, and agree in gender and number with it.

Ese reloj no. Páseme el reloj **suyo.**
*Not that watch. Hand me yours.*

Esta tierra es **mía,** dijo Ado.
*This land is mine, said Ado.*

✔ Stressed possessive adjectives can be used as possessive pronouns by eliminating the noun. In this instance the article and the possessive adjective must agree in gender and number with the noun that has been eliminated.

Señora López, **el pasaporte suyo** está vencido. **El suyo** está vencido.
*Your passport is expired, Mrs. López. Yours is expired.*

Necesito ver **la tarjeta suya,** señor Rivera. Necesito ver **la suya** también, señora López.
*I need to see your card, Mr. Rivera. I also need to see yours, Mrs. López.*

**3-4 Demonstrative adjectives** *are modifiers used to point out a specific person, place, thing or idea, and to distinguish it from others of the same class.*

✔ Demonstrative adjectives agree in gender and number with the noun they modify. They also precede it.

| singular | masculine | feminine |
|---|---|---|
| *this* | este | esta |
| *that* | ese | esa |
| *that (over there)* | aquel | aquella |

| plural | | |
|---|---|---|
| *these* | estos | estas |
| *those* | esos | esas |
| *those (over there)* | aquellos | aquellas |

**Este(a)/Estos(as)** refer to nouns that are near to the speaker in distance or time.

**Ese(a)/Esos(as)** refer to nouns that are farther away from the speaker in distance or time, but close to the listener.

**Aquel(la)/Aquellos(as)** refer to nouns that are quite far from the speaker and the listener in distance or time.

✔ Demonstrative adjectives differ from the demonstrative pronouns in that they have an accent mark on the stressed vowel: éste, ésa, aquélla.

Me gusta más **este** cuadro que **aquella** escultura.
*I like this picture better than that sculpture over there.*

Siempre recordaré **aquellos** años locos de los sesenta.
*I will always remember the crazy sixties. (those crazy years)*

**Esa** noche yo me enamoré.
*That night, I fell in love.*

**3-5 Adjectives of quantity** *are modifiers used to denote amount or quantity.*

| | |
|---|---|
| ¿cuánto(a)/¿cuántos(as)? | *how much, how many?* |
| poco(a)/pocos(as) | *little, few* |
| mucho(a)/muchos(as) | *a lot of, many* |
| otro(a)/otros(as) | *another* |
| demasiado(a)/demasiados(as) | *too much, too many* |
| bastante(s) | *enough* |
| tanto(a)/tantos(as) | *as much, as many* |
| vario(a)/varios(as) | *several* |

✔ Adjectives of quantity precede the noun.

**¿Cuántos** libros has leído?
*How many books have you read?*

He leído **muchas** novelas pero **pocos** dramas.
*I've read many novels, but few plays.*

¿Necesitas **otros** libros de teatro?
*Do you need other theater books?*

No, gracias. Préstame **otra** novela.
*No, thanks. Lend me another novel.*

¿Tienes **bastantes** bebidas?
*Do you have enough beverages?*

Sí, compré **varias** botellas de gaseosa y **varios** litros de limonada.
*Yes, I bought several bottles of soda and several liters of lemonade.*

**3-6 Indefinite adjectives** *refer to an undefined quantity of things or beings. They are less precise than the other adjectives of quantity.*

| singular | plural | |
|---|---|---|
| ningún | | *not any* |
| mismo(a) | mismos(as) | *same* |
| alguno(a) | algunos(as) | *some, a few* |
| | varios(as) | *several* |
| todo(a) | todos(as) | *all, any* |
| ninguno(a*) | ningunos(as*) | *not any* |
| algún | | *some* |
| tal | tales | *such* |
| cada | | *each, every* |

¿Les queda **alguna** duda?
*Do you have any more doubts?*

No, no nos queda **ninguna** duda.
*No, we do not have any doubts.*

**Cada** día la búsqueda de empleo se hace más difícil.
*The search for jobs becomes more difficult every day.*

Nunca he dicho **tal** cosa.
*I have never said that.*

*****ningunas** and **ningunos** are only used when the noun they modify is always used in the plural: **tijeras** *(scissors),* [tener] **ganas** *(to feel like doing something),* **vacaciones** *(holidays),* **anteojos**, **lentes**, or **gafas** *(glasses).*

No tengo **ningunas** ganas de verla.      **ningunas** vacaciones      **ningunos** anteojos
*I don't feel like seeing her.*      *no vacation*      *no glasses*

No encuentra **ningunos** lentes que vayan con su personalidad.
*He/She can't find any glasses that match her personality.*

## 3-7 Comparisons

### 3–7a Comparisons of equality

| tan<br>*as* | **+** | adjective<br>or adverb | **+** | como<br>*as* |
|---|---|---|---|---|
| tanto(a)/tantos(as)<br>*(as much, as many)* | **+** | noun | **+** | como<br>*as* |
| verb | **+** | tanto<br>*as much* | **+** | como<br>*as* |

**tan...como** is used to compare adjectives or adverbs. **Tan** is invariable and precedes the adjective or adverb. **Como** follows the adjective or adverb.

**tan +** adjective or adverb **+ como**

Mi trabajo es tan importante como el tuyo.
*My job is as important as yours.*

Hoy los tacos no están *tan* buenos **como** las empanadas.
*Today the tacos are not as good as the empanadas.*

Hoy los tacos no están **tan buenos**.
*Today the tacos are not so good.*

No hablo el español **tan bien como** Juan.
*I don't speak Spanish as well as Juan.*

✔ **Tanto** is an adjective when used to compare nouns. It agrees with the noun being compared.

*as    much/many   **noun**   as*

Tengo **tantas ilusiones como** tú.
*I have as many hopes as you.*

✔ **Tanto** is an adverb when used to compare verbs. As an adverb, it is invariable.

*verb* + **tanto como**

Duerme **tanto como** trabaja.
*He/She sleeps as much as he/she works.*

Elena estudia **tanto como** ellos.
*Elena studies as much as they.*

*the expression **tanto...como** can also mean *both. . . and*.

**Tanto** Tomás **como** Juan hablan español.
*Both Tomás and Juan speak Spanish.*

### 3-7b   Comparisons of inequality

✔ In Spanish, comparisons of inequality are made with **más que** *(more. . . than)* and **menos que** *(less/fewer. . . than)*.

| más (+) | + | adjective, adverb or noun | + | que *(than)* |
|---|---|---|---|---|
| menos (−) | + | adjective, adverb or noun | + | que *(than)* |
| más/menos | + | | + | de + number |
| verb | + | más/menos | + | que *(than)* |

**más**   *adjective*   **que**

La torta es **más** cara **que** el pan.
*The cake is more expensive than the bread.*

**menos**   *adverb*   **que**

Luis estudia **menos** seriamente **que** María.
*Luis studies less seriously than María.*

**menos**   *noun*   **que**

Tengo **menos** libros **que** tú.
*I have fewer books than you.*

*verb*   **más que**

Él trabaja **más que** usted.
*He works more than you.*

**Que** *(than)* is used for each expression except before numbers, where it is replaced by **de** *(than)*.

Me quedan **menos de** diez pesos.
*I have fewer than ten pesos left.*

✔ In negative sentences, **no tener más que** *(to have only)*, is used when referring to an exact or maximum amount.

En la vida **no tengo más que** un objetivo: soñar.
*I have only one goal in life: to dream.*

## 3–7c Adjectives with irregular comparative forms

✔ These adjectives have both a regular and an irregular comparative form, and the meaning is different in some cases.

| adjectives | regular | | irregular | |
|---|---|---|---|---|
| bueno | más bueno | | **mejor** | *better* |
| malo | más malo | | **peor** | *worse* |
| grande | más grande | *(larger)* | **mayor** | *older* |
| pequeño | más pequeño | *(smaller)* | **menor** | *younger* |

✔ **más bueno/más malo** refer primarily to the moral behavior or personality traits of people—usually goodness or the lack of it.

Juan es **más bueno** que Pedro.
*Juan is better/kinder than Pedro.*

Luis es **más malo** que su hermano.
*Luis is worse/meaner/naughtier than his brother.*

"Soy **más mala** que la peste", dijo Sierva María.
*"I am worse than the plague," Sierva María said.*

    (Gabriel García Márquez, *Del amor y otros demonios*)

✔ The irregular forms **mejor/peor** are used to describe physical abilities of people or the quality of things.

Es **mejor** jugador de fútbol que su amigo.
*He is a better soccer player than his friend.*

La tercera tormenta de nieve fue **peor** que la primera.
*The third snowstorm was worse than the first one.*

✔ **Más grande** and **más pequeño** are used to indicate size.

Mi casa es **más grande** que tu apartamento.
*My house is larger than your apartment.*

La cocina es **más pequeña** que la sala.
*The kitchen is smaller than the living room.*

✔ The irregular forms **mayor** and **menor,** when used with things, indicate a difference in degree or importance.

El problema de las drogas es **mayor** en la ciudad que en el campo.
*The problem with drugs is greater in the city than in the country.*

✔ **Mayor** and **menor,** when used to refer to people, communicate the idea of *old* or *older.*

Alejandro es **mayor** que Adam, pero Adam es **menor** que Pepita.
*Alejandro is older than Adam, but Adam is younger than Pepita.*

✔ The comparative forms of **nuevo** and **viejo** are used to describe the age of objects.

Mi auto es **más nuevo/viejo** que el de Juan.
*My car is newer/older than Juan's.*

**3-7d  The superlative of adjectives** is used to compare three or more people or things.
To form a superlative, add a definite article (**el, la, los, las**) before the comparative form.

$$\text{el, la, los, las } + \left\{ \begin{array}{lcl} \text{más} & \neq & \text{menos} \\ \text{mejor} & \neq & \text{peor} \\ \text{mayor} & \neq & \text{menor} \end{array} \right.$$

Este libro es **el mejor** que he leído.
*This is the best book I have ever read.*

Manolito: Soy **el más** alto, **el más** inteligente, **el más** listo y la persona **más** humilde del mundo.
*Manolito: I am the tallest, the most intelligent, the smartest, and the most humble person in the world.*

Mafalda: Eres **el mayor** mentiroso que he conocido en mi vida.
*Mafalda: You are the greatest liar that I have ever met.*

✘ The definite article is omitted when the superlative is placed after a noun preceded by a definite article or a possessive adjective.

María Callas fue **la cantante más** popular de su época.
*María Callas was the most popular singer of her time.*

Él es **su amigo más** fiel.
*He is his most loyal friend.*

| CHART 5 | IRREGULAR COMPARATIVE AND SUPERLATIVE FORMS | | |
|---|---|---|---|
| ADJECTIVE | ADVERB | COMPARATIVE | SUPERLATIVE |
| bueno | bien | mejor | el/la/los/las...mejor(es) |
| malo | mal | peor | el/la/los/las...peor(es) |
| grande | | mayor | el/la/los/las...mayor(es) |
| pequeño | | menor | el/la/los/las...menor(es) |
| mucho | mucho | más | el/la/los/las...más |
| poco | poco | menos | el/la/los/las...menos |

**3–7e  The absolute superlative** is used to denote an extreme degree of the trait described, without directly comparing the person or thing to anything else.

✔ The absolute superlative is formed by using an adverb to modify the adjective.

**muy** fácil   *very easy*       **muy** alto   *very tall*

An alternate way to convey the same meaning is by attaching the suffix -**ísimo(a)/-ísimos(as)** to the adjective.

✔ Attach the suffix directly when the adjective ends in a consonant.

popular → popular**ísimo**

✔ If the adjective ends in a vowel, drop the final vowel, and add -**ísimo(a)/-ísimos(as)**.

alto     → alt**ísimo**
grande → grand**ísimo**

✔ For adjectives ending in -**ble**, change -**ble** to -**bil** and add -**ísimo(a)/-ísimos(as)**.

*ble*       → **bil** + **ísimo** = **bilísimo**
ama-ble → ama-**bilísimo**

Orthographic changes are sometimes required when adding suffixes in order to maintain the original sound of a syllable.

**3-7f   Orthographic changes**

　　　c → qu　　　g → gu　　　z → c

c → qu
　　poco  → po**qu**ísimo   *little/very little*

g → gu
　　largo → lar**gu**ísimo   *long/very long*

z → c
　　feliz  → feli**c**ísimo   *happy/very happy*

✔ Adjectives with written accent marks drop them when -**ísimo** is attached.

fácil → facil**ísimo**   *easy/very easy*

# CHAPTER 4

## *Adverbs*

**ADVERBS** are words that qualify or modify verbs, adjectives, or other adverbs, and are invariable in form.

✔ Adverbs express manner, time, place, quantity, degree, doubt, affirmation, or negation.

**4-1 Adverbs of manner** *show the way in which a thing is done, or happens.*

✔ They are formed by adding the suffix **-mente** (equivalent to *-ly* in English) to the adjective.

✔ If the adjective ends in **-o**, change **-o** to **-a** and add **-mente**: **o → a + mente**

diario → diari**amente**   *daily*

✔ If the adjective ends in **-a, -e,** or a **consonant,** add the suffix **-mente** directly to the form.

entusiasta → entusiasta**mente**   *enthusiastically*
probable  → probable**mente**   *probably*

✔ If the adjective has a written accent mark, the accent remains on the adverb.

fácil  → fácil**mente**   *easily*
eficaz → eficaz**mente**   *effectively*

✔ When two or more adjectives occur in a series, add **-mente** only to the last one.

Remember to change adjectives ending in **-o** to **-a.**

Habla fuerte, clara y correcta**mente.**
*He/She speaks loudly, clearly, and correctly.*

✔ Often a prepositional phrase is preferable to an adverb.

Abrió la puerta **con cuidado.**          Abrió el libro **cuidadosamente.**
*He/She opened the door with care.*     *He/She opened the book carefully.*

## 4-2 Adverbs of time *place the action or event in time.*

✔ They answer the question **¿cuándo?** (*when?*).

| | | |
|---|---|---|
| ayer | anteayer | hoy |
| *yesterday* | *the day before yesterday* | *today* |
| mañana | pasado mañana | ahora |
| *tomorrow* | *the day after tomorrow* | *now* |
| enseguida | largo tiempo | antaño/en otro tiempo |
| *at once* | *for a long time* | *previously* |
| hace tiempo | hace poco | de ahora en adelante |
| *a long time ago* | *lately* | *from now on* |
| siempre | a menudo | a veces |
| *always* | *often* | *sometimes* |
| raramente | de pronto | primero |
| *rarely/seldom* | *suddenly* | *first(ly)* |
| luego | aún | de vez en cuando |
| *afterwards, later* | *still, yet* | *once in a while* |
| temprano | tarde | pronto |
| *early* | *late* | *soon* |
| inmediatamente | ya | entonces |
| *immediately, right now* | *now* | *then* |
| finalmente | desde antes | después/luego |
| *finally* | *since* | *then, later, afterwards* |

## 4-3 Adverbs of place *place the action or event in space.*

✔ Adverbs of place answer the question **¿dónde?** (*where?*).

**¿Dónde estás?**
*Where are you?*

**¿A dónde vas?**
*Where are you going?*

**¿Por dónde?**
*By where, through where?*

**¿Por dónde pasó?**
*Where did he/she pass by?*

**¿De dónde?**
*From where?*

**¿De dónde vienes?**
*Where do you come from?*

### Some adverbs of place

| | | | | |
|---|---|---|---|---|
| aquí<br>*here* | ahí<br>*there* | allí<br>*over there* | alto<br>*high* | bajo<br>*low* |
| encima de<br>*on, above* | debajo de<br>*underneath* | delante<br>*in front* | atrás<br>*behind* | dentro de<br>*inside* |
| fuera de<br>*outside* | adentro<br>*inside* | afuera<br>*outside* | lejos<br>*far* | cerca<br>*near* |
| en otra parte<br>*elsewhere* | en todas partes<br>*everywhere* | | | |

## 4-4 Adverbs of quantity *determine amount or quantity.*

✔ Adverbs of quantity answer the question **¿cuánto?** *(how much/many?).*

| | | | |
|---|---|---|---|
| todo<br>*totally* | nada<br>*nothing* | tanto<br>*so much* | algo<br>*something* |
| suficiente<br>*enough* | muy<br>*very* | tanto como<br>*as much, as many* | menos<br>*less* |
| mucho<br>*much, many* | poco<br>*little* | más<br>*more* | demasiado<br>*too much* |

## 4-5 Adverbs of doubt, affirmation, negation

**Doubt**

| | | | |
|---|---|---|---|
| quizás, tal vez<br>*maybe, perhaps* | probablemente<br>*probably* | aparentemente<br>*apparently* | |

**Affirmation**

| | | | |
|---|---|---|---|
| sí<br>*yes* | perfectamente<br>*perfectly* | sin duda<br>*no doubt, without a doubt* | también<br>*also* |
| por supuesto<br>*of course, sure* | cierto<br>*certain, true, agreed* | ciertamente<br>*certainly* | |

**Negation**

| | | | |
|---|---|---|---|
| no<br>*no* | ni<br>*nor* | de ningún modo<br>*in no way* | jamás<br>*never* |
| nadie<br>*nobody* | nada<br>*nothing* | tampoco<br>*neither* | nunca<br>*never* |

✔ To make a sentence negative, place the adverb **no** in front of the verb.

| | |
|---|---|
| John **no** habla español. | *John doesn't speak Spanish.* |
| **No** entiendo lo que usted dice. | *I don't understand what you are saying.* |
| **No** comprendo lo que dices. | *I don't understand what you say.* |
| **No** estoy de acuerdo contigo. | *I don't agree with you.* |
| **No** me gustó la película. | *I didn't like the movie.* |
| **No**, gracias. **No** quiero más. | *No thanks. I don't want more.* |

✔ If another negative adverb or word precedes the verb, (see Indefinites p. 117), **no** is not required.

| | |
|---|---|
| Hoy **no** vino **nadie** a clase. | *Nobody came to class today.* |

CHART 6    ADVERBS

| manner | affirmation | negation | time |
|---|---|---|---|
| adjective (ends in **-a**, **-e**, *or* if **-a consonant**) + *-mente* adjective (ends in o → **a**) + *-mente* | sí *yes* | no *no* | ahora/ahora mismo *now/right now* |
| así *like that* | perfectamente *perfectly* | de ningún modo *in no way* | antes *earlier* |
| bien *well* | cierto *certain* | nadie *nobody* | antaño *in days gone by* |
| mal *badly* | claro *clearly* | nunca *never* | anteayer *the day before yesterday* |
| mejor *better* | ciertamente *certainly* | ni *neither, nor* | a menudo *often* |
| peor *worse* | sin ninguna duda *without a doubt* | jamás *never* | a veces *sometimes* |
| **doubt** | por supuesto *sure, of course* | nada *nothing* | aún *still, yet* |
| quizás/tal vez *maybe, perhaps* | también *also* | tampoco *neither* | ayer *yesterday* |
| aparentemente *apparently* | sin duda *no doubt* | | de ahora en adelante *from now on* |
| probablemente *probably* | | | de pronto *suddenly* |

CHART 6          ADVERBS (continued)

| time | time | place | quantity |
|---|---|---|---|
| desde<br>*since* | raramente<br>*rarely, seldom* | aquí/ahí/allí<br>*here/there/over there* | cuánto<br>*how much, how many* |
| después/luego<br>*then, later,<br>afterwards* | siempre<br>*always* | acá/allá<br>*here/way over there* | algo<br>*a little, a bit* |
| enseguida<br>*at once* | tarde<br>*late* | encima/debajo<br>*on, above/under* | demasiado<br>*too much* |
| entonces<br>*then* | temprano<br>*early* | (a)delante/atrás<br>*in front/behind* | más<br>*more* |
| finalmente<br>*finally* | todavía<br>*still* | (a)dentro/(a)fuera<br>*inside/outside* | menos<br>*less* |
| hace poco<br>*recently* | todavía no<br>*not yet* | alrededor<br>*around* | muy<br>*very* |
| hace tiempo<br>*a long time ago* | ya/ya no<br>*already, now/no<br>longer* | alto/bajo<br>*high/loudly/low/softly* | mucho<br>*a lot, much* |
| hoy<br>*today* | de vez en cuando<br>*once in a while* | arriba/abajo<br>*up there/down there* | nada<br>*nothing* |
| inmediatamente<br>*immediately* | | encima/debajo<br>*on, above/ underneath* | poco<br>*a little* |
| largo tiempo<br>*for a long time* | | en frente/al fondo<br>*in front/in back* | suficiente<br>*enough* |
| mañana<br>*tomorrow* | | en otra parte<br>*elsewhere* | tanto<br>*so much* |
| pasado mañana<br>*the day after<br>tomorrow* | | en todas partes<br>*everywhere* | tanto como<br>*as much, as many* |
| primero<br>*first(ly)* | | lejos/cerca<br>*far/near* | |
| pronto<br>*soon* | | | |

# CHAPTER 5

## *Pronouns*

A **PRONOUN** takes the place of a noun.

**5-1** **Personal pronouns** *refer to people or things. A personal pronoun can be used as a subject, the direct or indirect object of a verb, or as the object of a preposition.*

| CHART 7 | | PERSONAL PRONOUNS: SUBJECT, DIRECT OBJECT, INDIRECT OBJECT | | | |
|---|---|---|---|---|---|

| SUBJECT | | DIRECT OBJECT | | INDIRECT OBJECT | |
|---|---|---|---|---|---|
| **yo** | *I* | **me** | *me* | **me** | *to/for me* |
| **tú** | *you (informal, singular)* | **te** | *you (informal, singular)* | **te** | *to/for you (informal, singular)* |
| **usted** | *you (formal, singular)* | **lo, la** | *you (formal, singular)* | **le** | *to/for you (formal, singular)* |
| **él** | *he/it* | **lo** | *him, it (masc.)* | **le** | *to/for him/her* |
| **ella** | *she/it* | **la** | *her, it (fem.)* | | |
| **nosotros(as)** | *we (masc./fem.)* | **nos** | *us* | **nos** | *to/for us* |
| **vosotros(as)** | *you (informal, plural)* | **os** | *you (informal, plural)* | **os** | *to/for you (informal, plural)* |
| **ustedes** | *you (formal, plural)* | **los, las** | *you (formal, plural)* | **les** | *to/for you (formal, plural)* |
| **ellos(as)** | *they (masc./fem.)* | **los** **las** | *them (masc.)* *them (fem.)* | **les** | *to/for them* |

*Note:* There is a great deal of variation in the use of third-person object pronouns in the Spanish-speaking world.

CHART 7          PERSONAL PRONOUNS: POSSESSIVE, REFLEXIVE, PREPOSITIONAL

| POSSESSIVE | REFLEXIVE | PREPOSITIONAL |
|---|---|---|
| **mío(a)/míos(as)** <br> *mine* | **me** <br> *myself* | **mí** <br> *me* <br> **-con**migo* |
| **tuyo(a)/tuyos(as)** <br> *yours (informal)* | **te** <br> *yourself* | **ti** <br> *you (informal, singular)* <br> **-contigo*** |
| **suyo(a)/suyos(as)** <br> *his/hers/its/yours (formal)* | **se** <br> *him-/her-/it-/yourself* <br> *(formal)* | **él/ella/usted** <br> *him/her/you (formal, singular)* <br> **-consigo*** |
| **nuestro(a)/nuestros(as)** <br> *ours* | **nos** <br> *ourselves* | **nosotros(as)** <br> *us* |
| **vuestro(a)/vuestros(as)** <br> *yours (informal)* | **os** <br> *yourselves (informal)* | **vosotros(as)** <br> *you (informal, plural)* |
| **suyo(a)/suyos(as)** <br> *theirs/yours (formal)* | **se** <br> *yourselves (formal)* | **ustedes** <br> *you (formal, plural)* |
| **suyo (a)/suyos (as)** <br> *theirs* | **se** <br> *themselves* | **ellos(as)** <br> *them* <br> **-consigo*** |

*__mí__ and **ti** combine with the preposition **con** (*with*) to form **conmigo** and **contigo**. Él, ella, ellos, and ellas combine with the preposition **con** (*with*) to form **consigo**.

**5-1a  Subject pronouns** identify the doer of the action and refer to people.

| singular | | plural | |
|---|---|---|---|
| **yo** | *I* | **nosotros(as)** | *we (masc./fem.)* |
| **tú** | *you (informal)* | **vosotros(as)** | *you (informal- masc./fem.)* |
| **usted** | *you (formal)* | **ustedes** | *you (formal)* |
| **él/ella** | *he/she* | **ellos(as)** | *they (masc./fem.)* |

**Tú** cantas muy bien.
*You sing very well.*

**Usted** es un gran pianista, Sr. Arrau.
*You are a great pianist, Mr. Arrau.*

**Ella** desayuna todas las mañanas.
*She has breakfast every morning.*

✔ It is not necessary to use the subject pronoun if the verb itself clarifies who is the subject of the sentence.

(**Nosotros**) Somos estudiantes de español.
*We are students of Spanish.*

> noun/pronoun + **yo** = **nosotros**
>
> noun/pronoun + **tú** = **ustedes**\*
>
> *but* **tú** y yo       = **nosotros**
>
> \*In Spain, **noun/pronoun + tú = vosotros**

✔ A subject pronoun can be used for clarification, contrast, or emphasis.

**Yo** soy muy soñadora; afortunadamente **él** es muy práctico.
*I am a dreamer; luckily he is very practical.*

**5-1b**    **Direct object pronouns** are pronouns that directly receive the action of the verb. They answer the questions *what?* or *whom?*

| singular | | plural | |
|----------|----------|----------|----------|
| **me** *me* | | **nos** *us* | |
| **te** *you (informal)* | | **os** *you (informal, plural)* | |
| **lo** *him*\* **la** *her*\* | | **los / las** *them* | |

\*it for objects

✔ Direct object pronouns replace a noun preceded by a definite or indefinite article, a possessive or a demonstrative adjective.

Necesito el/un/mi/este libro. Lo necesito.
*I need the/a/my/this book. I need it.*

✔ Direct object pronouns are placed directly before a conjugated verb.

¿Escribiste las cartas? Sí, las escribí.
*Did you write the letters? Yes, I wrote them.*

✔ Direct object pronouns appear after the word **no** when it appears.

¿Has leído El Quijote? No, **no** lo he leído.
*Have you ever read El Quijote? No, I have never read it.*

✔ Direct object pronouns may be attached to the end of an infinitive.

Hay que **leerlo** para mañana.
*It must be read for tomorrow./You must read it for tomorrow.*

✔ Direct object pronouns may be attached to a present participle (**-ing** form), or an affirmative command, with the addition of an accent mark.

Estamos **esperándolas** desde temprano en la mañana.
*We have been waiting for them since early this morning.*

¿El té? **Sírvalo,** por favor.
*The tea? Please, serve it now.*

✔ When an auxiliary verb precedes the infinitive or present participle, the direct object pronoun can be attached to the infinitive/present participle or precede the auxiliary. Both positions are acceptable.

Tenemos que leer**lo. Lo** tenemos que leer.
*We must read it.*

Estoy escribiéndo**la. La** estoy escribiendo.
*I am writing it.*

✔ The neuter direct object pronoun **lo** is used to refer back to an idea or concept already mentioned. Some verbs that usually add **lo** in this situation are: **decir, estar, pedir, preguntar, saber, ser.**

El profesor dijo que leyéramos El Quijote.     ¿Quién **lo** dijo? **Lo** dijo el profesor.
*The professor told us to read El Quijote.*     *Who said that? The professor said it.*

Juan está muy enfermo. Sí, **lo** sé.
*Juan is very sick. Yes, I know it.*

**5-1c**   **Indirect object pronouns** are pronouns that precede the direct object and usually answer the questions **to whom? to what?** or **for whom? for what?**

| singular | plural |
|---|---|
| **me** *to/for me* | **nos** *to/for us* |
| **te**  *to/for you* | **os**  *to/for you* |
| **le*** *to/for him/her*** | **les*** *to/for them*** |

*As previously mentioned, there is considerable variation in the forms used for the third person.
**the recipient of the direct object or the person or thing affected by the action.

✔ Indirect object pronouns are placed directly in front of a conjugated verb.

**Le** escribí una carta a papá.          Luis **me** envió una carta de amor.
*I wrote a letter to Daddy.*          *Luis sent a love letter to me.*

✔ Indirect object pronouns may be attached to the end of infinitives.

Hay que **pedirles** que guarden silencio.
*It must be asked of them to be quiet. (We must ask them to be quiet.)*

✔ Indirect object pronouns may be attached to present participles (-**ing** form), or affirmative commands, with the addition of an accent mark.

Estoy **pidiéndoles** que guarden silencio.
*I am asking them to be quiet.*

**Escríbame** apenas llegue.
*Write me as soon as you get there.*

✔ When an auxiliary verb precedes the infinitive or the present participle, the indirect object pronoun can be attached to the infinitive/present participle or precede the auxiliary.

**Les** estoy pidiendo que escuchen.
Estoy **pidiéndoles** que escuchen.
*I am asking them to listen.*

**Les** voy a pedir que lo compren.
Voy a **pedirles** que lo compren.
*I am going to ask them to buy it.*

**Common verbs that generally take an indirect object pronoun**

| | | | |
|---|---|---|---|
| contestar<br>*to answer* | dar<br>*to give* | decir<br>*to say* | doler*<br>*to hurt* |
| encantar*<br>*to delight* | enojar*<br>*to make angry* | explicar<br>*to explain* | faltar*<br>*to miss* |
| fascinar*<br>*to fascinate* | gustar*<br>*to please, to like* | importar*<br>*to care about* | interesar*<br>*to be interested in* |
| molestar*<br>*to annoy* | preguntar<br>*to ask* | regalar<br>*to give* | responder<br>*to answer* |

*These verbs are usually used in the third-person singular or plural. They always require an indirect object pronoun. The singular form is used with a singular noun or an infinitive; the plural form is used with a plural noun.

Me **gusta** la **clase** de español.
*I like my Spanish class. (The Spanish class pleases me).*

Me **encanta viajar.**
*I love to travel.*

¿Te **gustan** los **vinos** chilenos?
*Do you like Chilean wines?*

✔ To emphasize, contrast, or clarify, use **a** + the prepositional pronouns.

**A ti** te duele la cabeza pero **a mí** me duelen los pies.
*Your head hurts you, but my feet hurt me.*

**A ella** le interesa la literatura.
*She is interested in literature.*

## 5-1d Using direct and indirect object pronouns together

✔ When both an indirect and a direct object pronoun are used in a sentence, the indirect object pronoun always immediately precedes the object pronoun.

✔ The position of double object pronouns is the same as that of single object pronouns.

El camarero nos sirve la sopa.
*The waiter serves us the soup.*

El camarero **nos la** sirve.
*The waiter serves it to us.*

José está escribiendo una carta para ti.
*José is writing a letter for you.*

José está escribiéndo**tela**.
José **te la** está escribiendo.
*José is writing it to you.*

✔ If the indirect object pronouns **le** or **les** appear with the direct object pronouns **lo, los, la,** or **las**; change **le** or **les** to **se.**

Voy a enviarles un regalo a mis hijos.
*I am going to send my children a present.*

Voy a enviár**selo**.
*I am going to send it to them.*

Le voy a comprar un auto a mi hija.
*I am going to buy my daughter a car.*

**Se** lo voy a comprar.
*I am going to buy it for her.*

Tiempo de soñar es una novela poética, única, halógena. **Se la** recomiendo.
*Tiempo de soñar is a poetic, unique and halogenous novel. I recommend it to you.*

| CHART 8 | ORDER OF DIRECT AND INDIRECT PRONOUNS WHEN USED TOGETHER |
|---|---|

|  |  |  |  |  |
|---|---|---|---|---|
| me | lo |  |  |  |
| te | la |  |  |  |
| (no*) se | + los | + | verb |  |
| nos | las |  |  |  |
| os |  |  |  |  |

(no*) infinitive + indirect object + direct object

affirmative, imperative, and present progressive

verb + indirect object + direct object

*the negative adverb **no** precedes the pronouns in negative sentences.

**5-1e Prepositional pronouns** are pronouns used as objects of a preposition.

✔ They are identical to the subject pronouns with the exception of **mí** and **ti.**

| singular | | plural | |
|---|---|---|---|
| **mí** | *me* | **nosotros(as)** | *us* |
| **ti, usted** | *you* | **vosotros(as), ustedes** | *you* |
| **él/ella** | *him/her* | **ellos(as)** | *them* |

Las flores son para **mí**, los bombones para **ti**.
*The flowers are for me, the chocolates for you.*

Compré dulces para **ellos**.
*I bought them some candies.*

✔ **Mí** and **ti** combine with the preposition **con** to form **conmigo** and **contigo**.

Iré a la fiesta **contigo**.
*I will go to the party with you.*

**Contigo** pan y cebolla.
*All I need is you. (idiomatic expression)*

¿Quieres venir **conmigo**?
*Do you want to come with me?*

✔ After the prepositions **entre** *(between, among)*, **excepto** and **salvo** *(except)*, **según** *(according to)*, use the subject pronouns **yo** and **tú**, instead of **mí** and **ti**.

Entre **tú** y **yo**, no estudié mucho.
*Between you and me, I didn't study a lot.*

**Según** yo, este libro es excelente.
*According to me (in my opinion), this book is excellent.*

Todos fueron a la fiesta **excepto** tú y yo.
*Everyone went to the party, except for you and I.*

**5-1f** **Possessive pronouns** are pronouns that indicate possession.

| Definite article el/la/los/las +: | | | | |
|---|---|---|---|---|
| **singular** | | | **plural** | |
| ① **mío, mía** | *mine* | | **míos, mías** | *mine* |
| ② **nuestro(a)** | *ours* | | **nuestros(as)** | *ours* |
| ① **tuyo(a)** | *yours* | | **tuyos(as)** | *yours* |
| ② **vuestro(a)** | *yours* | | **vuestros(as)** | *yours* |
| ① **suyo(a)** | *his/hers/its* | | **suyos(as)** | *his/hers/its* |
| ② **suyo(a)** | *theirs* | | **suyos(as)** | *theirs* |

① Un poseedor

② Varios poseedores

✔ With definite articles, possessive pronouns are used to indicate the specific object possessed; their form indicates gender and number.

¿Es éste tu pasaporte? Sí, es **el mío.**
*Is this your passport? Yes, it is mine.*

Éstas son nuestras maletas.
*These are our suitcases.*

Éstas son **las nuestras.**
*These are ours.*

✔ After **ser** the definite article (**el, la, los, las**) may be omitted.

¿De quién es esta maleta? Es **mía.**
*Whose suitcase is this? It is mine.*

Las novelas son **mías.**
*The novels are mine.*

**5-1g** **Reflexive pronouns** indicate that the subject of a sentence does something to himself, herself, themselves. The subject of the action is also the recipient of the action.

| singular | | plural | |
|---|---|---|---|
| **me** | *to myself* | **nos** | *to ourselves* |
| **te** | *to yourself (informal)* | **os** | *to yourselves (informal)* |
| **se** | *to him-, her-, it-, yourself (formal)* | **se** | *to themselves, yourselves (formal)* |

Verbs that require the use of the reflexive pronouns are called reflexive verbs. For conjugation, see Verbs pp. 45–104.

✔ When the verb is conjugated, the reflexive pronoun precedes it.

(Yo) **Me** levanto tarde los domingos.
*I get up late on Sundays.*

Juan **se** lavó la cara.
*Juan washed his face.*

(Yo) **Me** maldije a **mí mismo.**
*I blamed myself.*

(Tú) **Te** lavas el pelo todos los días.
*You wash your hair every day.*

Note that **mí mismo** (*myself*) is used as in English to emphasize that the subject and object of the action are the same. When this fact is clear, **myself, himself,** etc. are omitted.

**Me** levanto a las seis.           *not:*
*I get up at six.*

Me levanto a **mí mismo** a las seis.
*I get myself up at six.*

✔ Reflexive pronouns are attached to the end of affirmative commands, present participles, and infinitives.

Levánta**te** a las siete.
*Get up at seven.*

Estamos poniéndo**nos** la ropa.
*We are getting dressed.*

Tengo que levantar**me** temprano.
*I must get up early.*

✔ Some verbs are always used with reflexive pronouns.

| | | | |
|---|---|---|---|
| acordarse | arrepentirse | arrodillarse | atreverse |
| *to remember* | *to repent* | *to kneel down* | *to dare* |
| burlarse | casarse | quejarse | suicidarse |
| *to make fun* | *to get married* | *to complain* | *to commit suicide* |

¿Te acuerdas de María?
*Do you remember María?*

Terminó la novela y luego se acostó.
*He/She finished the novel and then he/she went to bed.*

Se casaron y fueron muy felices.
*They got married, and lived happily ever after.*

The reflexive form in these verbs does not necessarily mean that the action is reflexive.

Se burló de nosotros.
*He made fun of us.*

**5-1h   Reciprocal pronouns** express the idea of doing something to each other.

   **nos**        **os**        **se**

Rita y su vecina **se ayudan.**          Siempre **nos vemos** en el verano.
*Rita and her neighbor help each other.*   *We always see each other in summer.*

✔ If the context is not clear, the reciprocal is indicated by **uno(a)/unos(as) al** otro(a)/a los otros(as).

Se defienden **uno al otro.**
*They defend each other.*

**5-1i   Relative pronouns** connect or relate two clauses and refer to a person or thing in the first clause.

| | | |
|---|---|---|
| **que** | **donde** | **(lo)(la) que/(lo)(la) cual** |
| **quien(es)** | **(el)(la) cual/(los)(las) cuales** | |
| **cuyo(a)/cuyos(as)** | **cuanto(a)/cuantos(as)** | |

✔ **Que;** meaning *that, which, who* or *whom;* is invariable and  may be used for people or objects. It can either be the subject or the direct object in the verb of the relative clause it introduces.

Tuve un examen de español. El examen duró dos horas.
*I had a Spanish test. The test lasted two hours.*

Tuve un examen de español **que** duró dos horas.
*I had a Spanish test that lasted two hours.*

Los estudiantes usan *Directo al grano.* Los estudiantes son muy inteligentes.
*The students use* Directo al grano. *The students are very intelligent.*

Los estudiantes **que** usan *Directo al grano* son muy inteligentes.
*The students who use* Directo al grano *are very intelligent.*

Los profesores hablan muy bien el español. Yo conozco a los profesores.
*The professors speak Spanish very well. I know the professors.*

Los profesores **que** yo conozco hablan muy bien el español.
*The professors whom I know speak Spanish very well.*

✔ **Donde,** meaning *where,* is invariable.

Quiero vivir **donde** pueda estar tranquilo.
*I want to live where I can be in peace.*

Ésta es la ventana por **donde** escaparon.
*This is the window through which they escaped.*

Caminemos hacia **donde** se pone el sol.
*Let's walk toward the place where the sun sets.*

✔ **El/La cual, los/las cuales,** meaning *which* (for things, ideas, or general situations), or *whom* (for people), are used in case of ambiguity to clarify the antecedent.

Ayer leí varios poemas, entre **los cuales** se hallaban dos de Neruda.
*Yesterday I read several poems; among them, two by Neruda.*

El profesor de español, con **el cual/el que*** hablamos ayer, es argentino.
*The Spanish professor, with whom we spoke yesterday, is Argentinian.*

La casa en **la cual/la que*** nos reunimos, tiene más de cien años.
*The house where we met is more than a hundred years old.*

*when the antecedent is introduced by the prepositions **a, de, con,** or **en; el/la cual, los/las cuales** can be replaced by **el/la, los/las...que.**

✔ **Quien(es),** meaning *who* or *whom,* refers only to people and is commonly used after a preposition (**a, de, con, para...**).

Estas son las personas **a quienes** me dirigí cuando llegué.
*These are the people whom I addressed when I got here.*

Es el autor **de quien** te hablé.
*He is the author I told you about.*

✔ **Lo que/lo cual**, meaning *what* or *that which*, are neuter forms and refer to a previous idea, event or situation.

Pepita dijo que entendía el subjuntivo, **lo cual/lo que** no nos extrañó.
*Pepita said that she understood the subjunctive, which didn't surprise us.*

✔ **Cuyo**, meaning *whose*, agrees in gender and number with the noun that follows it.

Es el autor **cuya** obra estudiamos en clase.
*He is the author whose work we studied in class.*

**5-1j   Demonstrative pronouns** replace the nouns to which they refer.

|  | masculine | feminine |  | neuter |
|---|---|---|---|---|
| *this one* | éste | ésta | *this* | esto |
| *these* | éstos | éstas | | |
| *that one* | ése | ésa | *that* | eso |
| *those* | ésos | ésas | | |
| *that one* | aquél | aquélla | *that* | aquello |
| *those* | aquéllos | aquéllas | | |

✔ **Éste** indicates proximity to the speaker.

✔ **Ése** indicates relative distance from the speaker.

✔ **Aquél** indicates that the person or thing pointed out is very distant from the speaker, in space or time.

Aquí hay varios estudiantes. **Éste** estudia filosofía, **ése**, español y **aquél**, medicina.
*Here we have several students. This one is studying philosophy, that one, Spanish, and that one over there, medicine.*

No me gustan estos zapatos, prefiero **aquéllos**.
*I don't like these shoes, I prefer those ones over there.*

**5-1k   Neuter demonstrative pronouns** refer to a general idea, statement or an object whose gender is unknown.

| **Esto** | **eso** | **aquello** |
|---|---|---|
| *this* | *that* | *that* |

Lo que me preocupa es que estudias muy poco. **Eso** es lo que me preocupa.
*What worries me is that you study so little. That is what worries me.*

¡**Aquello** fue inolvidable!          ¡**Esto** es fascinante!
*That was unforgettable!*          *This is fascinating!*

# CHAPTER 6

## *Verbs*

A **VERB** is a word, or a group of words, that expresses action, or a state of being.

✔ All Spanish **infinitives** end in **-ar, -er,** or **-ir.**

✔ Spanish verbs are conjugated by substituting the **-ar, -er,** or **-ir** ending for endings that correspond to reflect the subject doing the action.

✔ Verbs are classified according to the ending of the infinitive.

**-ar:** first conjugation verbs
**-er:** second conjugation verbs
**-ir:** third conjugation verbs

### 6-1  Uses of the infinitive

✔ Infinitives can function as nouns.

**El comer** calma la ansiedad.
*Eating calms anxiety.*

✔ Infinitives can appear as the object of a verb.

¿Qué <u>quieren</u> **hacer?**
*What do you want to do?*

✔ The infinitive can be the object of a preposition.

Antes <u>de</u> **comer,** lávate las manos.
*Wash your hands before eating.*

✔ The infinitive is used as the object of the verbs **escuchar, oír,** and **ver.**

¿Qué lástima!, no te vi **bailar.**
*What a pity! I didn't see you dance.*

✔ The infinitive is often used as a substitute for the imperative, to give instructions or directions.

Prohibido **estacionarse aquí.**
*It is forbidden to park here.*

✔ After **sin,** the infinitive indicates that an action has not yet occurred or has not been completed.

Se fueron sin **comer.**
*They left without eating.*

✔ Used after **al,** the infinitive means *on* or *upon doing* something.

Cierra la puerta **al salir.**
*Close the door upon leaving.*

**6-2** **Indicative** *is a mood used in ordinary objective statements.*

✔ The indicative is composed of the following tenses: present, present perfect, preterite, imperfect, pluperfect, past perfect, future, future perfect.

**6-3** **Present tense** *is used to express actions that occur in the actual moment, immediate future, or habitually. In this instance,* **tense** *means* **time.**

**6-3a   Present tense of first conjugation regular verbs: -ar**

✔ All regular **-ar** verbs follow the same pattern of conjugation; drop the **-ar** and add the following endings.

| **amar** | **(to love)** | | |
|---|---|---|---|
| **singular** | stem | | ending |
| yo | am | + | **-o** |
| tú | am | + | **-as** |
| usted/él/ella | am | + | **-a** |
| **plural** | | | |
| nosotros(as) | am | + | **-amos** |
| vosotros(as) | am | + | **-áis** |
| ustedes/ellos(as) | am | + | **-an** |

Common regular *-ar* verbs

| | | | | |
|---|---|---|---|---|
| am-**ar** | bail-**ar** | busc-**ar** | camin-**ar** | cant-**ar** |
| *to love* | *to dance* | *to look for* | *to walk* | *to sing* |
| contest-**ar** | convers-**ar** | dese-**ar** | enseñ-**ar** | esper-**ar** |
| *to answer* | *to chat, to talk* | *to want* | *to teach* | *to hope, to wait for* |
| estudi-**ar** | habl-**ar** | lleg-**ar** | llev-**ar** | mir-**ar** |
| *to study* | *to speak, talk* | *to arrive* | *to carry* | *to look at* |
| nad-**ar** | necesit-**ar** | practic-**ar** | pregunt-**ar** | trabaj-**ar** |
| *to swim* | *to need* | *to practice* | *to ask* | *to work* |

✔ Because verb endings indicate who the subject is, subject pronouns are generally omitted. Subject pronouns are usually only used in Spanish for clarification, emphasis, or contrast.

**Yo** soy alto y **ella** es baja.
*I am tall and she is short.*

✔ The present tense in Spanish has several equivalents in English: simple present, ongoing actions, and actions that will take place in the immediate future.

Hablamos español.
*We speak Spanish. We are speaking Spanish. We do speak Spanish.*

¿Hablamos español?
*Shall we speak Spanish?*

✔ The present tense can also express a habit.

Todos los días sueña conmigo.
*He/She dreams of me every day.*

✔ The present tense can also be used to soften a command.

¿Me pasas la sal, por favor?
*Would you hand me the salt, please?*

## 6–3b  Present tense of second conjugation regular verbs: -er

✔ All regular **-er** verbs follow the same pattern of conjugation: drop the **-er** and add the following endings.

| **comer** | *(to eat)* | | |
|---|---|---|---|
| **singular** | **stem** | | **ending** |
| yo | com | + | **-o** |
| tú | com | + | **-es** |
| usted/él/ella | com | + | **-e** |
| **plural** | | | |
| nosotros(as) | com | + | **-emos** |
| vosotros(as) | com | + | **-éis** |
| ustedes/ellos(as) | com | + | **-en** |

**Common regular** *-er* **verbs**

| | | |
|---|---|---|
| aprend-**er** | beb-**er** | com-**er** |
| *to learn* | *to drink* | *to eat* |
| comprend-**er** | corr-**er** | cre-**er** (en) |
| *to understand* | *to run* | *to think, to believe* |
| deb-**er** | deb-**er** + **infinitive** | le-**er** |
| *to owe* | *should, must; ought to do something* | *to read* |
| respond-**er** | vend-**er** | tos-**er** |
| *to answer* | *to sell* | *to cough* |

## 6-3c  Present tense of third conjugation regular verbs: -ir

✔ All regular **-ir** verbs follow the same pattern of conjugation: drop the **-ir** and add the following endings.

| **partir** | *(to leave)* | |
|---|---|---|
| **singular** | stem | ending |
| yo | part + | **-o** |
| tú | part + | **-es** |
| usted/él/ella | part + | **-e** |
| **plural** | | |
| nosotros(as) | part + | **-imos** |
| vosotros(as) | part + | **-ís** |
| ustedes/ellos(as) | part + | **-en** |

### Common regular *-ir* verbs

| | | |
|---|---|---|
| abr-**ir** | asist-**ir** (a) | decid-**ir** |
| *to open* | *to attend, go to* | *to decide* |
| describ-**ir** | discut-**ir** | escrib-**ir** |
| *to describe* | *to discuss* | *to write* |
| insist-**ir** (**en + infinitive**) | recib-**ir** | viv-**ir** |
| *to insist on* | *to receive, get* | *to live* |

## 6-3d  Present tense of stem-changing verbs: e → ie

✔ Changes occur in the singular forms and in the third person plural because these syllables are stressed.

| | | | |
|---|---|---|---|
| querer | pensar | preferir | entender |
| *to love, want* | *to think* | *to prefer* | *to understand* |
| comenzar | sentir | empezar | despertar(se) |
| *to start* | *to feel* | *to begin* | *to wake up* |
| perder | sentar(se) | cerrar | nevar |
| *to lose* | *to sit down* | *to close* | *to snow* |
| tener * | venir* | divertir(se) | entender |
| *to have* | *to come* | *to have fun* | *to understand* |

*****tener/venir** also have an irregular **yo** form: **tengo, vengo**

| comenzar | (to start/begin) | |
|---|---|---|
| **singular** | **stem** | **ending** |
| yo | comienz + | **-o** |
| tú | comienz + | **-as** |
| usted/él/ella | comienz + | **-a** |
| **plural** | | |
| nosotros(as) | comenz + | **-amos** |
| vosotros(as) | comenz + | **-áis** |
| ustedes/ellos(as) | comenz + | **-an** |

| querer | (to love, want) | |
|---|---|---|
| **singular** | **stem** | **ending** |
| yo | quier + | **-o** |
| tú | quier + | **-es** |
| usted/él/ella | quier + | **-e** |
| **plural** | | |
| nosotros(as) | quer + | **-emos** |
| vosotros(as) | quer + | **-éis** |
| ustedes/ellos(as) | quier + | **-en** |

## 6-3e   Present tense of stem-changing verbs: e → i

✔ Changes occur in the singular forms and in the third-person plural because these syllables are stressed.

| pedir<br>*to ask for* | despedir(se)<br>*to say goodbye* | servir<br>*to serve* | seguir<br>*to follow* |
|---|---|---|---|
| vestir(se)<br>*to dress, get dressed* | desvestir(se)<br>*to undress, get undressed* | decir*<br>*to say* | repetir<br>*to repeat* |

*decir also has an irregular **yo** form: **digo**

| pedir | (to ask for) | |
|---|---|---|
| **singular** | **stem** | **ending** |
| yo | pid + | **-o** |
| tú | pid + | **-es** |
| usted/él/ella | pid + | **-e** |
| **plural** | | |
| nosotros(as) | ped + | **-imos** |
| vosotros(as) | ped + | **-ís** |
| ustedes/ellos(as) | pid + | **-en** |

## 6-3f   Present tense of stem-changing verbs: o → ue

✔ Changes occur in the singular forms and in the third-person plural because these syllables are stressed.

| | | | | |
|---|---|---|---|---|
| almorzar<br>*to have lunch* | contar<br>*to count, tell* | poder<br>*can, be able* | probar<br>*to taste, try* | encontrar<br>*to find* |
| recordar<br>*to remember* | acordarse<br>*to remember* | volver<br>*to come back* | morir<br>*to die* | llover<br>*to rain* |
| dormir<br>*to sleep* | jugar<br>*to play* | resolver<br>*to resolve* | mostrar<br>*to show* | probar<br>*to taste* |

| contar<br>**singular** | *(to count, to tell)* o → ue<br>stem | ending |
|---|---|---|
| yo | cuent- | -o |
| tú | cuent- | -as |
| usted/él/ella | cuent- | -a |
| **plural** | | |
| nosotros(as) | cont- | -amos |
| vosotros(as) | cont- | -áis |
| ustedes/ellos(as) | cuent- | -an |

| jugar<br>**singular** | *(to play)* u → ue<br>stem | ending |
|---|---|---|
| yo | jueg + | -o |
| tú | jueg + | -as |
| usted/él/ella | jueg + | -a |
| **plural** | | |
| nosotros(as) | jug + | -amos |
| vosotros(as) | jug + | -áis |
| ustedes/ellos(as) | jueg + | -an |

**Jugar** is the only Spanish verb with **u → ue** stem change.

## 6-3g   Irregular verbs in the first-person singular

✔ The following verbs are irregular in the first-person singular of the present indicative, but regular in all other forms.

| hacer | hago (c changes to g) | *to do, to make* |
|---|---|---|
| dar | doy | *to give* |
| traer | traigo | *to bring* |
| oír | oigo | *to hear* |
| valer* | valgo | *to be worth* |
| conocer | conozco | *to know* |

| | | |
|---|---|---|
| producir | produzco | *to produce* |
| ver | veo | *to see* |
| saber | sé | *to know* |
| poner* | pongo | *to put* |
| salir* | salgo | *to leave* |

***valer**, **poner** and **salir** add a **g** between the stem and the final -**o**.

| hacer | | *(to do, to make)* | |
|---|---|---|---|
| **singular** | | stem | ending |
| yo | | hag + | -**o** |
| tú | | hac + | -**es** |
| usted/él/ella | | hac + | -**e** |
| **plural** | | | |
| nosotros(as) | | hac + | -**emos** |
| vosotros(as) | | hac + | -**éis** |
| ustedes/ellos(as) | | hac + | -**en** |

✔ Verbs ending in a vowel after you drop -**cer** or -**cir** from the infinitive add a **z** before the final **c** of the stem in the first-person singular.

| | | |
|---|---|---|
| cono-cer | conozco | *to know, be acquainted with* |
| tradu-cir | traduzco | *to translate* |
| estable-cer | establezco | *to establish* |
| ofre-cer | ofrezco | *to offer* |
| introdu-cir | introduzco | *to introduce* |
| produ-cir | produzco | *to produce* |

**6-3h  Other stem-changing verbs: ending in -ger, -gir, -guir, -uir, -iar, and -uar.**

✔ Verbs ending in -**ger**, -**gir** change the **g** of the stem to **j** in the first-person singular.

| | | |
|---|---|---|
| esco-ger | escojo | *to choose* |
| corre-gir | corrijo | *to correct* |

✔ Verbs ending in -**guir** change **gu** → **g**.

| | | |
|---|---|---|
| perse-**guir** | persigo | *to persecute* |

✔ Verbs ending in -**uir** add **y** to the stem in all the forms except the first- and second-person plural.

| concluir | | *(to conclude)* | |
|---|---|---|---|
| **singular** | | **plural** | |
| yo | concluyo | nosotros(as) | concluimos |
| tú | concluyes | vosotros(as) | concluís |
| usted/él/ella | concluye | ustedes/ellos/ellas | concluyen |

| | | | |
|---|---|---|---|
| atribuir<br>*to attribute* | construir<br>*to build* | contribuir<br>*to contribute* | destruir<br>*to destroy* |
| disminuir<br>*to decrease* | distribuir<br>*to distribute* | huir<br>*to flee* | excluir<br>*to exclude* |
| influir<br>*to influence* | obstruir<br>*to obstruct* | sustituir<br>*to substitute* | incluir<br>*to include* |

✔ Some verbs ending in **-iar** and **-uar** change **i → í** and **u → ú** in all the forms except the first- and second-person plural.

| **confiar** | | *(to trust, entrust)* | |
|---|---|---|---|
| **singular** | | **plural** | |
| yo | confío | nosotros(as) | confiamos |
| tú | confías | vosotros(as) | confiáis |
| usted/él/ella | confía | ellos/ellas | confían |

| | | | | |
|---|---|---|---|---|
| enviar<br>*to send* | espiar<br>*to spy* | guiar<br>*to guide* | resfriarse<br>*to catch a cold* | variar<br>*to vary* |

| **actuar** | | *(to act)* | |
|---|---|---|---|
| **singular** | | **plural** | |
| yo | actúo | nosotros(as) | actuamos |
| tú | actúas | vosotros(as) | actuáis |
| usted/él/ella | actúa | ellos/ellas | actúan |

| | | | |
|---|---|---|---|
| acentuar<br>*to stress, to*<br>*accentuate* | continuar<br>*to continue* | evaluar<br>*to evaluate* | graduarse<br>*to graduate* |

## 6-4 Present participle (Gerund): *a participle expressing present action.*

✔ The present participle corresponds to the **-ing** form in English.

✔ The present participle is formed by dropping the infinitive ending of the verb and adding **-ando** for **-ar** verbs and **-iendo** for **-er** and **-ir** verbs.

| minus | plus |
|---|---|
| -ar | -ando |
| -er | -iendo |
| -ir | -iendo |

✔ Verbs that are e → i stem-changing verbs in the present tense, maintain their stem change in the present participle.

> pedir      pidiendo     *(to ask)*

✔ In contrast, e → ie and o → ue stem-changing verbs do not retain their stem change in the present tense. They are conjugated like regular verbs, with the exception of the verbs below.

Exceptions

| | | | | |
|---|---|---|---|---|
| dormir | → | **durm** | + | -iendo | *to sleep* |
| morir | → | **mur** | + | -iendo | *to die* |
| poder | → | **pud** | + | -iendo | *to be able, can* |
| preferir | → | **prefir** | + | -iendo | *to prefer* |
| sentir | → | **sint** | + | -iendo | *to feel* |
| venir | → | **vin** | + | -iendo | *to come* |

✔ When the stem of an -er or -ir verb ends in a vowel, the i changes to y: **iendo → yendo**

| | | | |
|---|---|---|---|
| caer | → | cayendo | *to fall* |
| creer | → | creyendo | *to believe* |
| ir | → | yendo | *to go* |
| leer | → | leyendo | *to read* |
| oír | → | oyendo | *to hear* |
| traer | → | trayendo | *to bring* |

✔ The gerunds of the verbs **estar, ir,** and **venir** are not commonly used.

✔ The verbs **seguir** and **continuar + the gerund** show continuation of an action.

¿Tú **sigues trabajando** para la misma compañía?
*Are you still working for the same company?*

**Continúen leyendo,** por favor.
*Please, continue reading.*

✔ Object pronouns are attached to the present participle, and an accent mark is placed on the **a** or **e** of the gerund ending.

esperando a los niños     esperándolos
*waiting for the children*     *waiting for them*

leyendo el periódico     leyéndolo
*reading the newspaper*     *reading it*

✔ The present participle is usually equivalent to phrases in English that begin with **because, by, if, when,** or **while.**

Ahorramos tiempo usando el computador.
*We saved time by using the computer.*

Trabajando duro podremos realizar nuestros sueños.
*By working hard (If we work hard), we can accomplish our dreams.*

✔ After the main verb, the present participle expresses simultaneity and the idea of manner.

Siempre cenan **mirando** la televisión.
*They always have dinner while watching TV.*

Mis sueños los escribo **pensando** en ti.
*I write my dreams while thinking of you.*

✔ With verbs of perception, such as **escuchar** *(to listen)*, **oír** *(to hear)*, **mirar** *(to look at)*, **ver** *(to see)*, either the gerund or the infinitive can be used, as in English.

Los vi **saliendo/salir** del cine.
*I saw them leaving/leave the movies.*

Las escuchamos **hablando/hablar**.
*We listened to them talking/talk.*

✔ With **estar** to form progressive tenses, the present participle expresses an action already in progress.

**Estamos** trabajando.
*We are working.*

Cuando sonó el teléfono yo **estaba** estudiando.
*When the phone rang, I was studying.*

**6-5 The present progressive** *is used to describe an action that is taking place at the moment of speaking.*

✔ The present progressive is formed with the present of **estar** + the **present participle** of the verb.

✔ The equivalent in English is **to be** + the **-ing form** of the verb.

¿Qué **estás haciendo**?
*What are you doing?*

**Estoy estudiando.**
*I am studying.*

*Note:* You cannot use the Spanish present progressive the way you do the English present progressive. To express future actions in Spanish, use the present tense, the immediate future, or the future tense.

¿Cuándo **viajas**?
*When are you traveling?*

**Viajo** mañana.
*I am traveling tomorrow.*

¿Cuándo **vas a viajar**?
*When are you going to travel?*

¿Cuándo **viajarás**?
*When will you travel?*

**6-6 The present perfect (pretérito perfecto)** *is a verb tense that expresses an action or state completed at the time of speaking.*

✔ The present perfect tense indicates that an action has been finished in the very recent past.

✔ The present perfect is formed by adding the present tense form of the auxiliary verb **haber** to the past participle of the verb.

|  |  |  |  | -ar | -er | -ir |
|---|---|---|---|---|---|---|
| yo | **he** | verb stem | + | -ado | -ido | -ido |
| tú | **has** | verb stem | + | -ado | -ido | -ido |
| usted/él/ella | **ha** | verb stem | + | -ado | -ido | -ido |
| nosotros(as) | **hemos** | verb stem | + | -ado | -ido | -ido |
| vosotros(as) | **habéis** | verb stem | + | -ado | -ido | -ido |
| ustedes/ellos(as) | **han** | verb stem | + | -ado | -ido | -ido |

**6-7** **The past participle** *form of the verb implies completion. That is, the action described by the verb is completed with respect to a specific point in time.*

✔ The **past participle** of Spanish verbs is formed by adding the suffix **-ado** to the stem of **-ar** verbs, and the suffix **-ido** to the stem of **-er** and **-ir** verbs.

| -ar | -er | -ir |
|---|---|---|
| + **-ado** | + **-ido** or **-ído** if the stem ends in **-a, -e** or **-o** | + **-ido** or **-ído** if the stem ends in **-a, -e** or **-o** |
| am-**ado** | s-**ido**    le-**ído** | viv-**ido** |

✔ The past participle is used much the way it is in English:

Siempre **hemos querido** a los animales.
*We **have** always **loved** animals.*

Le **he dado** mi coche.
*I **have given** him my car.*

**Verbs with an irregular past participle**

| abrir | → | abierto | *to open* | cubrir * | → | cubierto | *to cover* |
|---|---|---|---|---|---|---|---|
| decir | → | dicho | *to say* | escribir* | → | escrito | *to write* |
| hacer* | → | hecho | *to do/make* | imprimir | → | impreso | *to print* |
| morir | → | muerto | *to die* | poner* | → | puesto | *to put* |
| romper | → | roto | *to break* | volver* | → | vuelto | *to return* |
| ver* | → | *to see* | visto | | | | |

*and their compounds

Adiós, te **he amado** hasta la locura. **He abierto** mi corazón a una nueva pasión.
*Good-bye; I loved you madly. I have opened my heart to a new passion.*

✔ When the past participle is used as an adjective, it must agree in gender and number with the noun it is modifying.

La ventana está **rota**.  
*The window is broken.*

Las puer**tas** están cerra**das**.  
*The doors are closed.*

✔ Some verbs have two forms for the past participle. The regular form is used to form the compound tenses; the irregular form is used as an adjective.

| verb | regular | irregular |
|------|---------|-----------|
| confundir<br>*to confuse, mistake* | confundido | confuso |
| despertar<br>*to wake up* | despertado | despierto |
| elegir<br>*to elect, choose* | elegido | electo |
| prender<br>*to catch, seize, turn on* | prendido | preso |
| soltar<br>*to release, untie* | soltado | suelto |
| sustituir<br>*to substitute* | sustituido | sustituto |

Estoy **confundido**.  
*I am confused.*

La explicación es muy **confusa**.  
*The explanation is very confusing.*

Los niños aún no se han **despertado**.  
*The kids have not woken up yet.*

Los niños son muy **despiertos**.  
*The kids are very alert.*

Fui **elegido** presidente de mi clase.  
*I was elected president of my class.*

El presidente **electo** viajará mañana a Washington.  
*The president elect will travel to Washington tomorrow.*

**6-8  The preterite** *is a tense used to express a past action.*

✔ The preterite focuses on the beginning, the ending, or the completed act.

**6-8a  Preterite of regular verbs**

| subject | verb endings | | |
| | -ar | -er | -ir |
| --- | --- | --- | --- |
| yo | -é | -í | -í |
| tú | -aste | -iste | -iste |
| usted/él/ella | -ó | -ió | -ió |
| nosotros(as) | -amos | -imos | -imos |
| vosotros(as) | -asteis | -isteis | -isteis |
| ustedes/ellos(as) | -aron | -ieron | -ieron |

**hablar** *(to speak)*

| singular | | plural | |
| --- | --- | --- | --- |
| yo | habl -é | nosotros(as) | habl -amos |
| tú | habl -aste | vosotros(as) | habl -asteis |
| usted/él/ella | habl -ó | ustedes/ellos(as) | habl -aron |

**6–8b  The preterite of verbs with spelling changes**

✔ Verbs ending in -ar and -er, with stem changes in the present tense, do not have stem changes in the preterite.

✔ -ir verbs that are stem-changing in the present tense (o → ue, e → ie, e→ i) only change in the third-person singular and plural in the preterite.

**dormir** *(to sleep)*

| singular | | plural | |
| --- | --- | --- | --- |
| yo | dormí | nosotros(as) | dormimos |
| tú | dormiste | vosotros(as) | dormisteis |
| usted/él/ella | durmió | ustedes/ellos(as) | durmieron |

**pedir** *(to ask for, to order)*

| singular | | plural | |
| --- | --- | --- | --- |
| yo | pedí | nosotros(as) | pedimos |
| tú | pediste | vosotros(as) | pedisteis |
| usted/él/ella | pidió | ustedes/ellos(as) | pidieron |

✔ To maintain the sound of the infinitive, verbs ending in **-car, -gar,** and **-zar** undergo a spelling change in the first-person singular of the preterite.

| -car | c | $\rightarrow$ | changes to | $\rightarrow$ | **qu** | $\rightarrow$ | buscar | busqué | *to look for* |
|------|---|---|---|---|---|---|---|---|---|
| -gar | g | $\rightarrow$ | changes to | $\rightarrow$ | **gu** | $\rightarrow$ | jugar | jugué | *to play* |
| -zar | z | $\rightarrow$ | changes to | $\rightarrow$ | **c** | $\rightarrow$ | abrazar | abracé | *to embrace* |

✔ **-ir** and **-er** verbs that have a vowel before the infinitive ending change the **i** to **y** in the third-person singular and plural in the preterite.

**leer** *(to read)*

| singular | | plural | |
|---|---|---|---|
| yo | leí | nosotros(as) | leímos |
| tú | leíste | vosotros(as) | leisteis |
| usted/él/ella | leyó | ustedes/ellos(as) | leyeron |

### 6-8c  The preterite of irregular verbs

✔ Irregular verbs in the preterite have an irregular stem based on the first-person singular. The first-person singular ends in an unstressed **e**; the third-person singular in an unstressed **o**.

| singular | plural |
|---|---|
| -e | -imos |
| -iste | -isteis |
| -o | -ieron |

| | | | | | |
|---|---|---|---|---|---|
| andar | **anduv-** + endings | *to walk* | poder | **pud-** + endings | *can* |
| estar | **estuv-** + endings | *to be* | poner | **pus-** + endings | *to put* |
| tener | **tuv-** + endings | *to have* | saber | **sup-** + endings | *to know* |
| caber | **cup-** + endings | *to fit* | querer | **quis-** + endings | *to want* |
| haber | **hub-** + endings | *to have* | venir | **vin-** + endings | *to come* |

✔ The following are irregular verbs that differ slightly from the verbs above because their stems end in **j**. For these verbs, drop the **i** of the third-person plural ending.

| singular | plural |
|---|---|
| -e | -imos |
| -iste | -isteis |
| -o | -eron |

| | | |
|---|---|---|
| decir | **dij-** + endings | *to say* |
| traer | **traj-** + endings | *to bring* |
| conducir | **conduj-** + endings | *to drive* |
| producir | **produj-** + endings | *to produce* |

Hernán y Elisa nos condujeron al cine.
*Hernán and Elisa drove us to the theater.*

| | **dar** *(to give)* | **hacer** *(to do)* | **ser/ir** *(to be/to go)* |
|---|---|---|---|
| **singular** | | | |
| yo | di | hice | fui |
| tú | diste | hiciste | fuiste |
| usted/él/ella | dio | hizo | fue |
| **plural** | | | |
| nosotros(as) | dimos | hicimos | fuimos |
| vosotros(as) | disteis | hicisteis | fuisteis |
| ustedes/ellos(as) | dieron | hicieron | fueron |

✔ **Ser** and **ir** have identical forms in the preterite. The context clarifies the meaning.

Juan **fue** a escuchar a Claudio Arrau.          El concierto **fue** excelente.
*Juan went to listen to Claudio Arrau.*          *The concert was excellent.*

## 6–8d  Uses of the preterite

✔ The preterite is used to indicate that an action or event began or ended in the past.

Al subir el telón **comenzó** la obra.          Las clases **terminaron** la semana pasada.
*As the curtains went up, the play began.*          *Classes ended last week.*

✔ The preterite is used to indicate a series of actions or events that were completed in the past.

**Me levanté** a las seis, **desayuné** y **salí** para la universidad.
*I got up at six, had breakfast, and left for school.*

✔ The preterite can express repeated past action, if such repeated action is considered as a complete unit.

**Hablé** con Juan seis veces la semana pasada.
*I spoke with Juan six times last week.*

✔ The preterite indicates a completed act or event.

Lo **compré** en Santiago.          La conferencia **se realizó** ayer.
*I bought it in Santiago.*          *The conference was held yesterday.*

✔ The preterite is used when telling a story to narrate the completed actions that develop the story line.

Estaba soñando al borde de la playa, las olas mojaban mis pies, cuando su voz me **invitó** a galopar por el fondo del océano.
*I was dreaming near the beach, the waves wetting my feet, when her/his voice invited me to gallop in the depths of the ocean.*

✔ The preterite can indicate physical or mental condition, or a state of mind in the past, if viewed as completed.

Ayer **estuve** muy enferma.      Luis **estuvo** de mal humor todo el día.
*Yesterday I was very sick.*      *Luis was in a bad mood all day long.*

✔ The preterite is used to break the continuity of an ongoing activity.

Caminábamos por la playa cuando **comenzó** a llover.
*We were walking on the beach when it started to rain.*

**6-9** **The imperfect** *is a tense used to designate, in the past, an action or a condition as incomplete, continuous, or coincident with another action.*

✔ The imperfect is equivalent to three English verb forms.

Yo **trabajaba** en Argentina.
*I worked/used to work/was working in Argentina.*

### 6–9a  Imperfect of regular verbs

| drop: | -ar | -er | -ir |
|---|---|---|---|
| **add endings:** | | | |
| yo | -aba | -ía | -ía |
| tú | -abas | -ías | -ías |
| usted/él/ella | -aba | -ía | -ía |
| nosotros(as) | -ábamos | -íamos | -íamos |
| vosotros(as) | -abais | -íais | -íais |
| ustedes/ellos(as) | -aban | -ían | -ían |

### 6-9b  The imperfect of irregular verbs

✔ There are only three irregular verbs in the imperfect.

| | ir *(to go)* | ser *(to be)* | ver *(to see)* |
|---|---|---|---|
| **singular** | | | |
| yo | iba | era | veía |
| tú | ibas | eras | veías |
| usted/él/ella | iba | era | veía |
| **plural** | | | |
| nosotros(as) | íbamos | éramos | veíamos |
| vosotros(as) | ibais | erais | veíais |
| ustedes/ellos(as) | iban | eran | veían |

## 6-9c Uses of the imperfect

✔ The imperfect is used to tell time in the past and to express age.

**Eran** las ocho en punto cuando la obra comenzó.
*It was eight o'clock when the play began.*

Alejandro **tenía** cuatro años cuando dio su primer recital de piano. *Alejandro was four years old when he gave his first piano recital.*

✔ The imperfect describes states of mind and feelings in the past. State of being verbs denote no movement or change: **estar, parecer, querer, ser, etc.**

María **estaba** contenta de terminar el curso.
*María was happy to finish the course.*

✔ The imperfect is used to describe people, actions, situations, weather, or things in the past.

Mi madre **era** alta y delgada.            **Tocaba** el piano.
*My mother was tall and slender.*       *She used to play the piano.*

En su último concierto la sala **estaba** llena, y eso que **estaba** lloviendo a cántaros.
*At her last concert the theater was full, even though it was raining cats and dogs.*

✔ Use the imperfect to describe repeated habitual actions in the past.

Siempre **íbamos** de vacaciones a Boquerón.
*We always used to go to Boquerón on vacation.*

✔ The imperfect is used to describe two or more simultaneous past actions in progress: used with **mientras** (*while*) or with **cuando** (*when*), when **cuando** is used in the sense of *while*.

No se haga el tonto compadre, usted **leía** por sobre mi hombro mientras yo **escribía** ¡E il orbo era rondo!, le dijo Chavalillo a Sempronio.
*Don't be silly, my pal, you were reading over my shoulder while I was writing ¡E il orbo era rondo!, Chavalillo told Sempronio.*

(Gustavo Gac-Artigas, *¡E il orbo era rondo!*)

Cuando **estábamos** en la escuela **estudiábamos** todos los días y **sacábamos** buenas notas.
*When we were in school we used to study every day and we got good grades.*

✔ Use the imperfect in indirect discourse when the verb of the main clause is in the past.

El profeta dijo que **estaba** destinado a morir.
*The prophet said that he was destined to die.*

✔ The imperfect is used to begin a story.

Había/Érase una vez...
*Once upon a time there was...*

## 6-10 Preterite vs. Imperfect

The preterite and imperfect tenses are two ways of expressing past actions and events, but each tense is used within a specific context and follows specific criteria. Sometimes, the choice of one or the other tense depends on the speaker's point of view. In general, the preterite is associated with the expression of actions completed in the past, while the imperfect is used to describe routine actions and states of being in the past.

✔ The imperfect and the preterite serve different functions when telling a story in the past.

### 6-10a The imperfect sets the scene.

✔ External conditions, such as time, date, weather, etc. are usually expressed with the imperfect.

**Eran** las diez de la mañana de un hermoso día de verano. **Hacía** calor y el sol **brillaba** en medio del cielo azul. María y los niños **paseaban** por el parque.
*It was ten o'clock in the morning on a beautiful summer day. It was hot, and the sun was shining in the center of the blue sky. María and the children were strolling in the park.*

✔ Use the imperfect to describe the characters' appearance, age, physical traits, feelings, etc.

Ella **era** joven y bonita; **llevaba** una blusa blanca y una falda rosada. Los niños, quienes **tenían** cuatro y cinco años,...
*She was young and pretty, and was wearing a white blouse with a pink skirt. The children, who were four and five years old,...*

✔ The imperfect is used to describe background activities, such as what was going on, or what people were doing.

...**jugaban** felices cerca de un árbol, **mientras** María **leía** un libro en un banco.
*...were playing happily near a tree, while María was reading a book on a bench.*

### 6-10b The preterite relates the actions that develop the story line.

✔ The actions were completed in the past, and they are specific, not continuous or descriptive.

De pronto, uno de los niños **comenzó** a gritar. María **corrió** para ver qué pasaba. Cuando **llegó** a donde estaban los niños, **vio** que el menor, Julito, lloraba colgando de la rama del árbol.
*Suddenly, one of the children started screaming. María ran to find out what was going on. When she arrived at the place where the children were playing, she saw that the youngest one, Julito, was crying, hanging from a tree branch.*

In some situations, either the preterite or the imperfect may be used, depending on how the speaker sees the action or series of actions.

## Imperfect

✔ Habitual or repetitive action.

1) Juanita **trabajaba** todo el día.
   *Juanita used to work all day long.*

2) En verano **íbamos** a la playa todos los días.
   *In the summer we used to go to the beach every day.*

3) Cuando era estudiante universitaria, todos los días **desayunaba, tomaba** mis libros y **me iba** a la universidad.
   *When I was a college student, I used to have breakfast, get my books, and leave for school.*

✔ Description of physical or mental condition or state of mind.

Anoche **tenía** fiebre.
*Yesterday night I had a fever.*

Juan **se sentía** muy feliz por la noticia.
*Juan was feeling very happy because of the news.*

✔ In indirect discourse, use the imperfect for the conversation that's being reported indirectly.

Don Eduardo dijo que **estaba** cansado.
*Don Eduardo said that he was tired.*

El director dijo que no **era** necesario llegar tan temprano.
*The director said that it was not necessary to arrive so early.*

✔ The imperfect describes simultaneous actions seen as ongoing in the past.

Mientras Roberto **leía** la novela, José **escribía** una carta y nosotros **mirábamos** la televisión.
*While Roberto was reading the novel, José was writing a letter, and we were watching TV.*

✔ When action in progress is interrupted by another action, the imperfect is used to describe the action in progress.

Cuando **caminábamos** por la calle, Juan se nos acercó.
*When we were walking down the street, Juan approached us.*

✔ When action in progress is contrasted to a completed action, the imperfect is used for the action in progress.

Mientras Roberto leía, Juan hizo su tarea.
*Juan did his homework while Roberto was reading.*

# Preterite

✔ Use the preterite to express an action seen as a completed unit.

Juanita **trabajó** todo el día.
*Juanita worked all day.*

En verano **fuimos** a la playa todos los días.
*In the summer we went to the beach every day.*

Esta mañana **desayuné, tomé** mis libros y **me fui** a la universidad.
*This morning I had breakfast, got my books, and left for school.*

✔ The preterite expresses a physical or mental condition or state of mind, viewed as completed.

Anoche tuve fiebre toda la noche.
*Last night I had a fever all night long. (I have no fever now.)*

Juan **se sintió** muy triste por la noticia.
*Juan felt very sad because of the news. (He doesn't feel sad anymore.)*

✔ In indirect discourse, use the preterite for the verb that is expressing the relationship between the subject and the quote.

Don Eduardo **dijo** que estaba cansado.
*Don Eduardo said that he was tired.*

El director **dijo** que no era necesario llegar tan temprano.
*The director said that it was not necessary to arrive so early.*

*Note:* Some other common relating verbs are **confirmar** (*to confirm*) **contestar/responder** (*to answer*), **preguntar** (*to ask*).

✔ The preterite describes completed actions begun at the same time in the past.

Mientras Roberto **leyó** la novela, José **escribió** una carta y nosotros **miramos** la televisión.
*While Roberto read the novel, José wrote a letter, and we watched TV.*

✔ The action that interrupts the action in progress takes the preterite.

Cuando caminábamos por la calle, Juan **se nos acercó**.
*When we were walking down the street, Juan approached us.*

✔ The preterite is used for the completed action that took place against the background of the ongoing action.

Mientras Roberto leía, Juan **hizo** su tarea.
*Juan did his homework while Roberto was reading.*

## 6-11 Verbs with different meaning *in the preterite and the imperfect*

### conocer

✔ In the preterite, **conocer** means *met.*

**Conocí** a mi esposo en París.
*I met my husband in Paris.*

✔ In the imperfect, **conocer** means *knew, was acquainted with.*

No **conocía** la poesía de Neruda hasta que estudié español.
*I didn't know Neruda's poetry until I studied Spanish.*

### saber

✔ In the preterite, **saber** means *found out,* or *learned.*

María, al leer la carta, **supo** que había aprobado el examen.
*When María read the letter, she learned that she had passed the test.*

✔ In the imperfect, **saber** means *knew about, had knowledge of.*

No **sabía** que Gabriela Mistral había ganado el Nóbel.
*I didn't know that Gabriela Mistral had won a Nobel prize.*

### poder

✔ When **poder** is used affirmatively in the preterite, it means *succeeded in.*

Por fin **pude** convencer a Daniela de que tenía razón.
*Finally, I succeeded in convincing Daniela that she was right.*

✔ When **poder** is used negatively in the preterite, it means *failed to.*

Juan no **pudo** pasar el examen.
*Juan failed to pass the exam.*

✔ In the imperfect, **poder** means *was (not) able to* regardless of whether it is used affirmatively or negatively.

Pepita no **podía** correr.
*Pepita was not able to run.*

### querer

✔ When **querer** is used affirmatively in the preterite, it means *tried,* or *attempted to.*

**Quise** llamarte antes pero no pude.
*I tried to call you before, but I couldn't.*

✔ When **querer** is used negatively in the preterite, it means *refused.*

María no **quiso** escucharme.
*María refused to listen to me.*

✔ In the imperfect, **querer** means *wanted (didn't want),* regardless of whether it is used affirmatively or negatively.

Pedro no **quería** ser abogado, **quería** ser pintor.
*Pedro didn't want to be a lawyer; he wanted to be a painter.*

## haber

✔ In the preterite, **haber** means *there was (were)* in the sense of *happened.*

**Hubo** un accidente en la mina.
*There was an accident in the mine.*

✔ In the imperfect, **haber** means *there was (were)* in the sense of *there existed.*

**Había** restos humanos en la mina.
*There were human remains in the mine.*

## tener

✔ In the preterite, **tener** means *got.*

**Tuve** una A en español.
*I got an A in Spanish.*

✔ In the imperfect, **tener** means *had.*

José **tenía** mucho trabajo que hacer.
*José had a lot of work to do.*

**6-12 The past progressive** *is a tense used to express or describe an action that was in progress at a specific moment in the past.*

✔ The past progressive is formed with the imperfect of **estar** + present participle of the verb.

$$\left.\begin{array}{l} \text{estaba} \\ \text{estabas} \\ \text{estaba} \\ \text{estábamos} \\ \text{estabais} \\ \text{estaban} \end{array}\right\} + \quad \text{present participle}$$

**Estabas estudiando** cuando llegó Josefa.
*You were studying when Josefa arrived.*

**6-13 The past perfect** *is a tense used to describe an action that was completed before another action in the past.*

✔ The past perfect is formed by combining the imperfect of **haber + the past participle** of the verb.

**singular**

| yo | había | |
|---|---|---|
| tú | habías | } + past participle |
| usted/él/ella | había | |

**plural**

| nosotros(as) | habíamos | |
|---|---|---|
| vosotros(as) | habíais | } + past participle |
| ustedes/ellos(as) | habían | |

Los niños ya **habían salido** cuando tú llamaste.
*The children had already left when you called.*

**6-14 The future tense** *is a tense that expresses actions that have not yet occurred.*

✔ The English equivalent is **will/shall + verb.**

¿Qué **harás** mañana? **Iré** al cine.
*What will you do tomorrow? I will go to the movies.*

✔ The future can also be used to express probability or to make conjectures in the present.

Luis está ausente. ¿**Estará** enfermo?
*Luis is absent. I wonder if he is sick. He might be sick.*

✔ **Deber de** in the present + **infinitive** also expresses probability.

**Deben de** ser las ocho.
*It might be eight o'clock.*

## 6-14a Future tense of regular verbs

✔ Attach the following endings to the infinitive.

| singular | plural |
|----------|--------|
| -é | -emos |
| -ás | -éis |
| -á | -án |

**estar** *(to be)*

**singular**

| subject | stem | ending |
|---------|------|--------|
| yo | estar | -é |
| tú | estar | -ás |
| usted/él/ella | estar | -á |

**plural**

| | | |
|---------|------|--------|
| nosotros(as) | estar | -emos |
| vosotros(as) | estar | -éis |
| ustedes/ellos(as) | estar | -án |

**ser** *(to be)*

**singular**

| subject | stem | ending |
|---------|------|--------|
| yo | ser | -é |
| tú | ser | -ás |
| usted/él/ella | ser | -á |

**plural**

| | | |
|---------|------|--------|
| nosotros(as) | ser | -emos |
| vosotros(as) | ser | -éis |
| ustedes/ellos(as) | ser | -án |

**ir** *(to go)*

**singular**

| subject | stem | ending |
|---------|------|--------|
| yo | ir | -é |
| tú | ir | -ás |
| usted/él/ella | ir | -á |

**plural**

| | | |
|---------|------|--------|
| nosotros(as) | ir | -emos |
| vosotros(as) | ir | -éis |
| ustedes/ellos(as) | ir | -án |

## 6-14b  Future tense of verbs with altered stems

✔ The future tense of verbs with altered stems is formed by adding the regular future endings to irregular stems.

- **verbs that drop *e* from the infinitive**

| | | | |
|---|---|---|---|
| *to have* | haber | **habr-** | habré |
| *to be able* | poder | **podr-** | podré |
| *to want* | querer | **querr-** | querré |
| *to know* | saber | **sabr-** | sabré |

- **verbs that change *e* or *i* in the infinitive → *d***

| | | | |
|---|---|---|---|
| *to put* | poner/d | **pondr-** | pondré |
| *to leave* | salir/d | **saldr-** | saldré |
| *to have* | tener/d | **tendr-** | tendré |
| *to come* | venir/d | **vendr-** | vendré |

- **verbs that drop the *c* and the *e* from the infinitive**

| | | | |
|---|---|---|---|
| *to say* | decir | **dir-** | diré |
| *to do/make* | hacer | **har-** | haré |

*Note:* the future tense of the impersonal **hay** is **habrá**.

## 6-15  **The near future** *is used to express future actions or events in the near future.*

✔ The English equivalent to the near future is **to be going + infinitive.**

✔ The near future is formed by the **present of ir + a + infinitive**

| | | | |
|---|---|---|---|
| yo | voy | a | |
| tú | vas | a | |
| usted/él/ella | va | a | |
| nosotros(as) | vamos | a | + infinitive |
| vosotros(as) | vais | a | |
| ustedes/ellos | van | a | |

¿Qué **van a** tocar en el concierto?
*What are you going to play at the concert?*

**Vamos a** tocar una pieza de Enrique Granados.
*We are going to play a piece by Enrique Granados.*

## 6-16  **The future perfect** *is a compound tense that indicates an action will take place in the future, and be completed after another action in the future has taken place.*

✔ The future perfect is formed with the future of **haber + the past participle.**

✔ The future perfect corresponds to **will have + past participle.**

habré
habrás
habrá
habremos
habréis
habrán
} + past participle

Gustavo **habrá terminado** su búsqueda de la felicidad cuando encuentre la puerta de entrada a Cíbola, la ciudad perdida.
*Gustavo will have finished his search for happiness when he finds the entrance to Cíbola, the lost city.*

**6-17 The conditional** *is a mood that expresses a hypothetical situation.*

✔ The conditional has two tenses: conditional present and conditional perfect. It tells what *would* happen in future actions, or in the case of **deber,** what *should* happen.

No, ese invento no **funcionaría.**
*No, that invention would not work.*

✔ **Deber de** in the imperfect **+ infinitive** may be used to express probability in the past.

**Debían de** ser las diez. *(Serían las diez.)*
*It was probably ten o'clock.*

**6-17a The present conditional of regular verbs**

✔ The present conditional is formed by adding the following endings to the complete infinitive of **-ar, -er,** and **-ir** verbs.

<u>estar</u>                 *(to be)*

**singular**

| subject | stem | ending | plural | | |
|---------|------|--------|--------|------|--------|
| yo | estar | -ía | nosotros(as) | estar | -íamos |
| tú | estar | -ías | vosotros(as) | estar | -íais |
| usted/él/ella | estar | -ía | ustedes/ellos(as) | estar | -ían |

✔ All verbs are regular in the conditional with the exception of those verbs that form the future on an irregular stem. The irregular stems that are used in the future tense are also used for the conditional.

- **verbs that drop *e* from the infinitive**

| | | | |
|---|---|---|---|
| to *have* | haber | **habr** | habría |
| to *be able* | poder | **podr** | podría |
| to *want* | querer | **querr** | querría |
| to *know* | saber | **sabr** | sabría |

- **verbs that change *e* or *i* in the infinitive → *d***

| | | | |
|---|---|---|---|
| to *put* | poner/d | **pondr** | pondría |
| to *leave* | salir/d | **saldr** | saldría |
| to *have* | tener/d | **tendr** | tendría |
| to *come* | venir/d | **vendr** | vendría |

- **verbs that drop the *c* and the *e* from the infinitive**

| | | | |
|---|---|---|---|
| to *say* | decir | **dir** | diría |
| to *do/make* | hacer | **har** | haría |

*Note:* the conditional tense of the impersonal **hay** is **habría**.

✔ The present conditional is used with the past subjunctive to speculate about the present in sentences containing **si** *(if)* clauses.

**Si** tuviera más tiempo **estudiaría** otros idiomas.
*If I had more time, I would study other languages.*

✔ The conditional expresses probability or conjecture regarding the past, usually with the verbs **estar, haber, ser,** and **tener.**

El poeta **tendría** unos setenta años cuando murió.
*The poet must have been about seventy when he died.*

✔ The conditional is used in subordinated clauses after main verbs of communication, knowledge, or belief (**decir, saber, creer,** etc.). It expresses a future probability in relation to a time in the past.

**Creí** que **ganarías** el premio Planeta.
*I thought that you would win the Planeta prize.*

**Ayer me dijeron** que **serías** un gran pianista.
*Yesterday they told me that you would be a great pianist.*

✔ The conditional is used to soften requests or commands.

¿**Podría** traerme el libro?          ¿Me **ayudarías** a terminar?
*Would you bring me the book?*          *Would you help me finish?*

¿**Podrían** guardar silencio, por favor?
*Would you be quiet, please?*

**6-17b  The conditional perfect** is used to express what would have occurred at a moment in the past.

✔ The conditional perfect is formed with the conditional forms of **haber + the past participle** of the verb.

✔ The conditional perfect corresponds to **would have + past participle.**

$$
\text{habr} \; + \;
\left.
\begin{array}{l}
\text{-ía} \\
\text{-ías} \\
\text{-ía} \\
\text{-íamos} \\
\text{-íais} \\
\text{-ían}
\end{array}
\right\}
\; + \text{ past participle}
$$

✔ The conditional perfect is used with the pluperfect subjunctive to speculate about the past.

Juan **habría ido** al concierto si hubiera conseguido boletos.
*Juan would have gone to the concert if he had gotten tickets.*

**Los alumnos habrían tenido** que estudiar *Directo al grano* para pasar brillantemente
el examen.
*The students would have had to study* Directo al grano *in order to pass the exam brilliantly.*

✔ The conditional perfect refers to a future action in relation to the past.

El dijo que para junio ya **habría terminado** sus estudios.
*He said that he would have finished school by June.*

| Chart 9 | Agreement between the tenses in hypothetical systems |
|---|---|

| Condition | Result |
|---|---|
| **present** | **future** |
| Si **tengo** tiempo | iré al cine. |
| *If I have time* | *I will go to the movies.* |
| **imperfect subjunctive** | **conditional present** |
| Si **tuviera** tiempo | iría al cine. |
| *If I had time* | *I would go to the movies.* |
| **pluperfect subjunctive** | **conditional perfect or pluperfect subjunctive** |
| Si **hubiera tenido** tiempo | **habría/hubiera** ido al cine. |
| *If I had had time* | *I would have gone to the movies.* |

**6-18 The subjunctive** *is a verbal mood that expresses the attitude the speaker has toward a fact or action. Primarily it indicates that the outcome is uncertain.*

✔ It has four tenses.

| | | |
|---|---|---|
| present subjunctive | **cante** | *that I sing* |
| imperfect subjunctive | **cantara** | *that I sang* |
| present perfect subjunctive | **haya cantado** | *that I have sung* |
| pluperfect subjunctive | **hubiera cantado** | *that I had sung* |

✔ The subjunctive is used to express doubt, desire, emotion, hope, possibility, influence, nonexistence, or uncertainty.

✔ It represents contingent or hypothetical situations, actions viewed subjectively, or subordinate statements.

✔ The dependent clause contains the verb in the subjunctive and is often introduced by **que**. It is usually subordinated to another idea in the form of an independent clause containing the verb in the indicative mood.

✔ There are four conditions that call for the use of the subjunctive:

**volition**    **emotion**    **unreality**    **doubt** and/or **denial**

### 6–18a Uses of the subjunctive

✔ Any sentence that expresses doubt, willingness, a request, a suggestion, a command, a judgement or emotion in the principal clause will require the subjunctive in the subordinate clause. The subordinate clause is often introduced by **que**.

**Main clause** *(indicative)* **+ que + dependent clause** *(subjunctive)*

Les sugiero que se levanten temprano.
*I suggest you get up early.*

✔ In repetitive structures the subjunctive is used to express contradiction or submission.

**Haga** lo que **haga** no me darán el ascenso.
*No matter what I do, they will not give me the promotion.*

✔ To form the present subjunctive of regular verbs:

(**-ar**) -e/-es/-e/-emos/-éis/-en

first-person present indicative minus -o + endings.

(**-er**/**-ir**) -a/-as/-a/-amos/-áis/-an

## 6-18b Volition

✔ willingness:

| | | | | |
|---|---|---|---|---|
| aconsejar* | desear | esperar | exigir* | insistir en |
| *to advise* | *to wish* | *to hope* | *to demand* | *to insist on* |
| necesitar | ordenar | pedir | permitir* | preferir |
| *to need* | *to command* | *to ask someone to do something* | *to allow* | *to prefer* |
| prohibir* | querer | recomendar* | rogar* | sugerir* |
| *to forbid* | *to want* | *to recommend* | *to beg* | *to suggest* |

*These verbs can also be followed by an infinitive without a change in meaning.

Les prohibo **que vayan** al cine.
*I forbid you to go to the movies.*

Les prohibo **ir** al cine.
*I forbid you to go to the movies.*

✔ These verbs of volition express the preferences, wishes, suggestions, requests, and implied command of the speaker.

**Le exijo** que **llegue** a tiempo.
*I require that you arrive on time.*

**Les sugiero** que **dejen** de fumar.
*I suggest you stop smoking.*

**Te aconsejo** que **estudies** para el examen.
*I advise you to study for the exam.*

**Te ruego** que **te cuides.**
*I beg you to take care of yourself.*

**Les recomiendo** que **hagan** ejercicio todos los días.
*I recommend they exercise every day.*

## 6-18c Ojalá

Ojalá, meaning *I* or *we hope*, and *I* or *we wish*, may be used with or without **que** and is followed by the subjunctive.

**Ojalá** (que) **te den** el empleo.
*I hope that they give you the job.*

## 6-18d Emotion

| | | | | |
|---|---|---|---|---|
| alegrarse de | avergonzarse | esperar | entristecer | temer |
| *to be happy* | *to be ashamed* | *to hope* | *to sadden* | *to fear* |
| lamentar | sorprender | apenarse | sentir | |
| *to regret* | *to surprise* | *to feel sorrow* | *to be sorry* | |

**Me alegro de** que **hayan terminado** a tiempo.
*I am happy that you finished on time.*

✔ Note that the subject in the main clause differs from the subject in the subordinate clause.

**Me apena (a mí)** que **(tú)** no **puedas** acompañarme.
*I feel sorry that you cannot come with me.*

**Me alegro (yo)** de que **(nosotros) estemos** de vacaciones.
*I am happy that we are on vacation.*

**Esperamos (nosotros)** que el médico **(él) llegue** a tiempo.
*We hope that the doctor will arrive on time.*

*Note:* If there is no subject change, an infinitive is used instead of a subjunctive clause.

Me alegro de **poder** ir de vacaciones.
*I am happy to be able to go on vacation.*

### 6-18e  Doubt and denial

| | | | |
|---|---|---|---|
| dudar<br>*to doubt* | negar<br>*to deny* | no creer<br>*not to believe* | no parecer<br>*not to seem* |
| ser probable<br>*to be probable* | no pensar<br>*not to think* | no ser verdad<br>*not to be true* | no ser seguro<br>*not to be sure* |
| quizás<br>*it may be* | no ser cierto<br>*not to be true* | puede ser<br>*perhaps* | tal vez<br>*maybe* |

**Dudo** que Juan **diga** el secreto.     **No creo** que **regreses** a tu país.
*I doubt that Juan will reveal the secret.*     *I don't think that you will return to your country.*

✔ The verbs **creer** *(to believe)*, parecer *(to seem, to look)* and **pensar** *(to think)* are followed by the subjunctive only when used in the negative, when doubt is implied.

**No creo** que Juan **venga** a verte.     Yo creo que sí vendrá.
*I don't believe that Juan will come to see you.*     *I do believe that he will come.*

### 6-18f  The subjunctive with *tal vez* and *quizás*

✔ The expressions **tal vez** and **quizás,** meaning *perhaps* or *maybe,* are followed by the subjunctive to express doubt or uncertainty.

**Tal vez me gradúe** el año próximo.     **Quizás te llame** por teléfono.
*Maybe I will graduate next year.*     *Maybe I'll call you.*

### 6-18g  Unreality: indefiniteness and nonexistence

### Subjunctive in adjective clauses

✔ When a clause is used as an adjective to describe a person, place, or thing, the verb can be in the indicative or subjunctive mood.

✔ Use the subjunctive if the antecedent is indefinite, nonexistent, or hypothetical.

¿Hay aquí una persona que **sepa** pintar?
*Is there someone here who knows how to paint?*

Quiero comprar una casa que **tenga** seis habitaciones.
*I want to buy a house that has six rooms.*

✔ Use the subunctive if the antecedent is negative.

No encuentro ningún libro que **hable** de los Mayas.
*I cannot find a book that tells about the Mayas.*

✔ Use the indicative if the antecedent is definite, specific, or known to exist.

Busco a la persona que **sabe** pintar.
*I am looking for the person who knows how to paint.*

Quiero comprar la casa que **tiene** seis habitaciones.
*I want to buy the house that has six rooms.*

✔ In addition to **que**, words such as **quien** and **donde** can introduce adjective clauses.

¿Existirá algún país **donde** pueda ser feliz?
*I wonder if there is a country in which I can be happy.*

Juan quería un padre con **quien** pudiera hablar.
*Juan wanted a father whom he could talk to.*

## 6-18h  Subjunctive with impersonal expressions

✔ The subjunctive is used to express judgments and opinions.

| | | | | |
|---|---|---|---|---|
| es ridículo<br>*it is ridiculous* | es importante<br>*it is important* | es bueno<br>*it is good* | es malo<br>*it is bad* | es necesario<br>*it is necessary* |
| es curioso<br>*it is curious* | es inútil<br>*it is useless* | es probable<br>*it is probable* | es extraño<br>*it is strange* | es mejor<br>*it is better* |
| es lógico<br>*it is logical* | es fácil<br>*it is easy* | es posible<br>*it is possible* | es una pena<br>*it is a pity* | es raro<br>*it is odd* |
| es triste<br>*it is sad* | es dudoso<br>*it is doubtful* | es urgente<br>*it is urgent* | es difícil<br>*it is difficult* | es imposible<br>*it is impossible* |
| es deseable<br>*it is desirable* | es fantástico<br>*it is fantastic* | es una lástima<br>*it is a pity* | es una maravilla<br>*it is a wonder* | es preciso<br>*it is necessary* |

**Es una pena** que no **dejes** de fumar.
*It is a pity/shame that you don't stop smoking.*

**Es importante** que **vayas** al laboratorio de idiomas.
*It is important for you to go to the language lab.*

**Es urgente** que **veamos** al médico.
*It is urgent that we see the doctor.*

**Es bueno** que **estudien** otros idiomas.
*It is good that they study other languages.*

**Es malo**, *e ilegal*, que **copien** un libro sin la autorización del autor.
*It is wrong, and illegal, to make copies of a book without the author's permission.*

✔ However if the subject of the sentence is neither expressed nor implied, the expressions shown above are followed by an infinitive.

**Es importante ir** al laboratorio de idiomas.
*It is important to go to the language lab.*

✔ If the impersonal expression in the main clause expresses a certainty (**es obvio, es cierto, es seguro, es verdad**), then the indicative is used in the subordinate clause.

**Es obvio** que Luis **está** enamorado.
*It is obvious that Luis is in love.*

## 6-18i Subjunctive in adverb clauses

| | | |
|---|---|---|
| para que | a fin (de) que | sin que |
| *so that* | *in order that* | *without* |
| a menos que/a no ser que/salvo que | antes (de) que | con tal (de) que |
| *unless* | *before* | *provided that* |
| en caso (de) que | siempre que | de manera que |
| *in case* | *as long as* | *so that* |
| a condición (de) que | | |
| *on the condition that* | | |

✔ The previous expressions are used to relate an event or an action that is indefinite or uncertain; it may or may not take place. These expressions are always followed by the subjunctive.

Te compré el libro para que lo **estudies**.
*I bought you the book so that you can study it.*

✔ The **subjunctive** follows the **conjunctions of time** shown in the table when they introduce forthcoming events or hypothetical actions.

| | | | |
|---|---|---|---|
| en cuanto<br>*as soon as* | cuando<br>*when* | mientras<br>*while* | después (de) que<br>*after* |
| aunque<br>*although,*<br>*even though* | hasta que<br>*until* | tan pronto (como)<br>*as soon as* | |

**Future action:**

Estudiará cuando **llegue** a casa.      Tan pronto como **llegue**, le entregaré la carta.
*He will study when he gets home.*      *As soon as he arrives, I will give him the letter.*

**Hypothetical:**

Escribiré aunque **tenga** que dejar de enseñar.
*I will write even if I must stop teaching.*

✔ The previous conjunctions of time require the indicative when they refer to an action that has happened, is happening, or habitually happens.

**Habitual:**

Siempre estudia cuando **llega** a casa.
*He always studies when ge gets home.*

**Actual:**

Escribo aunque **enseño** todos los días.
*I write although I teach every day.*

**Past:**

Fue al estadio aunque **llovía** a cántaros.
*He went to the stadium even though it was raining cats and dogs.*

## 6-19 Present subjunctive

✔ The present subjunctive of regular verbs is formed by deleting the final **-o** of the first-person singular of the present indicative and adding the endings indicated.

| | -ar | -er | -ir |
|---|---|---|---|
| **singular** | | | |
| | -e | -a | -a |
| | -es | -as | -as |
| | -e | -a | -a |
| **plural** | | | |
| | -emos | -amos | -amos |
| | -éis | -áis | -áis |
| | -en | -an | -an |

✔ Some verbs normally considered irregular are not considered irregular in the present subjunctive because the **yo** form of the present indicative is used as the stem of the present subjunctive.

| | infinitive | present indicative | present subjunctive |
|---|---|---|---|
| *to have* | tener | tengo | **tenga** |
| *to do/make* | hacer | hago | **haga** |
| *to say* | decir | digo | **diga** |

## 6-19a Present subjunctive of stem-changing verbs

✔ The subjunctive forms of **-ar** and **-er** stem-changing verbs have the same pattern as that of the present indicative.

| -ar, -er | e → ie | o → ue |
|---|---|---|

| -ar | e → ie |
|---|---|

| | | | |
|---|---|---|---|
| pensar<br>*to think* | comenzar<br>*to begin* | empezar<br>*to begin, start* | nevar<br>*to snow* |
| sentàrse<br>*to sit down* | cerrar<br>*to close* | despertarse<br>*to wake oneself up* | |

**-ar      o → ue**

| | | | |
|---|---|---|---|
| almorzar<br>*to have lunch* | acordar(se)<br>*to remember* | contar<br>*to count, tell* | encontrar<br>*to find* |
| jugar<br>*to play* | probar<br>*to try, test* | recordar<br>*to remember* | |

**-er      e → ie**

| | | |
|---|---|---|
| entender<br>*to understand* | perder<br>*to lose* | querer<br>*to want* |

**-er      o → ue**

| | | |
|---|---|---|
| llover<br>*to rain* | poder<br>*to be able* | volver<br>*to return* |

**cerrar** *(to close)*

| | Present indicative | Present subjunctive |
|---|---|---|
| yo | cierro | cierre |
| tú | cierras | cierres |
| usted/él/ella | cierra | cierre |
| nosotros(as) | cerramos | cerremos |
| vosotros(as) | cerráis | cerréis |
| ustedes/ellos(as) | cierran | cierren |

**volver** *(to return)*

| | Present indicative | Present subjunctive |
|---|---|---|
| yo | vuelvo | vuelva |
| tú | vuelves | vuelvas |
| usted/él/ella | vuelve | vuelva |
| nosotros(as) | volvemos | volvamos |
| vosotros(as) | volvéis | volváis |
| ustedes/ellos(as) | vuelven | vuelvan |

✔ -ir stem-changing verbs such as **preferir** (e → ie) and **dormir** (o → ue) undergo the same changes in both the present indicative and the present subjunctive, except in the **nosotros** and **vosotros** forms. In these forms the unstressed e of the stem changes to i (**preferir, sentir**) and the unstressed **o** changes to **u** (**dormir, morir**) in the present subjunctive. Compare the tenses in the chart that follows.

**preferir**   (*to prefer*)   (e → ie)

|  | Present indicative | Present subjunctive |
| --- | --- | --- |
| yo | prefiero | prefiera |
| tú | prefieres | prefieras |
| usted/él/ella | prefiere | prefiera |
| nosotros(as) | preferimos | prefiramos |
| vosotros(as) | preferís | prefiráis |
| ustedes/ellos(as) | prefieren | prefieran |

**dormir**   (*to sleep*)   (o → ue)

|  | Present indicative | Present subjunctive |
| --- | --- | --- |
| yo | duermo | duerma |
| tú | duermes | duermas |
| usted/él/ella | duerme | duerma |
| nosotros(as) | dormimos | durmamos |
| vosotros(as) | dormís | durmáis |
| ustedes/ellos(as) | duermen | duerman |

✔ **-ir** stem-changing verbs such as **repetir** (e → i) have the same stem change in all the forms in the present subjunctive.

| yo | repita |
| --- | --- |
| tú | repitas |
| usted/él/ella | repita |
| nosotros(as) | repitamos |
| vosotros(as) | repitáis |
| ustedes/ellos(as) | repitan |

Other verbs of this type appear below.

**-ir**   (e → i)

| pedir | despedir(se) | reír(se) | repetir |
| --- | --- | --- | --- |
| *to ask for* | *to say good-bye* | *to laugh* | *to repeat* |
| servir | vestir(se) | desvestir(se) | |
| *to serve* | *to dress, get dressed* | *to undress, get undressed* | |

### 6-19b Verbs with irregular subjunctive forms

✔ There are six Spanish verbs that have irregular forms in the present subjunctive because their stems are not based on the **yo** form of the present indicative.

|  | **dar** *(to give)* | **estar** *(to be)* | **haber** *(to have)* |
|---|---|---|---|
| yo | dé* | esté | haya |
| tú | des | estés | hayas |
| usted/él/ella | dé* | esté | haya |
| nosotros(as) | demos | estemos | hayamos |
| vosotros(as) | deis | estéis | hayáis |
| ustedes/ellos(as) | den | estén | hayan |

*The accents on the first- and third-person singular forms of **dar** are necessary to distinguish them from the preposition **de.**

|  | **ir** *(to go)* | **saber** *(to know)* | **ser** *(to be)* |
|---|---|---|---|
| yo | vaya | sepa | sea |
| tú | vayas | sepas | seas |
| usted/él/ella | vaya | sepa | sea |
| nosotros(as) | vayamos | sepamos | seamos |
| vosotros(as) | vayáis | sepáis | seáis |
| ustedes/ellos(as) | vayan | sepan | sean |

✔ In order to maintain the sounds corresponding to the letters **-c**, **-g**, and **-z** (**k, g, s**), the stems of verbs that end in **-car, -gar** and **-zar** have spelling changes in all the forms of the present subjunctive.

**sacar**   c → qu
saque, saques, saqu...

**pagar**   g → gu
pague, pagues, pagu...

**empezar**   z → c
empiece, empieces, empiece...

## 6-20 Present perfect subjunctive

✔ The present perfect subjunctive is used in the same way as the present perfect in English, but in sentences that require the subjunctive in the subordinate clause.

✔ The present perfect subjunctive is formed by using the present subjunctive of the auxiliary verb **haber + a past participle.**

haya
hayas
haya
hayamos
hayáis
hayan
} + past participle

haya cantado   *that I have sung*

✔ Subordinate clauses requiring the subjunctive use the present perfect subjunctive if the verb in the main clause is in the present or future tense.

Espero que hayas **visitado el museo.**
*I hope that you have visited the museum.*

✔ If the action in the subordinate clause occurs prior to the time expressed in the main clause or the time implied by the speaker, the present perfect subjunctive is used.

Compraré otro auto cuando **haya vendido** el viejo.
*I will buy a new car once I have sold the old one.*

✔ With expressions like **ojalá, quizás, tal vez,** use the present perfect subjunctive.

Ojalá que **te hayas ganado** el premio.
*I hope you have won the prize.*

**6-21 Imperfect subjunctive** *The past imperfect subjunctive has the same uses as the present subjunctive, except that it relates actions or events that took place in the past.*

✔ The imperfect subjunctive of **-ar, -er,** and **-ir** verbs is formed by using the **ellos** form of the preterite tense indicative, subtracting the **-ron** ending and adding the following endings.

-ra      -ramos
-ras     -rais
-ra      -ran

The variant form that follows is more commonly used in literature.

-se      -semos
-ses     -seis
-se      -sen

cantara or **cantase**   *that I sang*

✔ Note that the **nosotros** form has an accent mark on the vowel before the ending **-ramos** or   **-semos.**

cantáramos/cantásemos, comiéramos/comiésemos

✔ All the verbs that are irregular in the preterite are irregular in the imperfect subjunctive. See preterite of irregular verbs on page 58.

### 6-21a  Uses of the imperfect subjunctive

✔ The imperfect subjunctive is used after **ojalá** (*I wish* or *I hope*) to express your wishes about the future.

Ojalá que no **tuviéramos** huracanes este año.
*I wish that we would not have any hurricanes this year.*

✔ The imperfect subjunctive is used after **como si** (*as if*) because it always indicates a statement contrary to fact.

Juan habla **como si fuera** el Presidente.
*Juan talks as if he were the President.*

✔ The imperfect subjunctive is used after **quién** to express a personal wish in an impersonal way.

**¡Quién supiera** cantar!
*I wish I could sing!*

✔ The imperfect subjunctive is used when the verb in the main clause is in the past (preterite, imperfect, pluperfect), and requires the subjunctive in the subordinate clause.

Ana afirmó que cuando **se casara** lo haría con un hombre que **fuera** inteligente y que **tuviera** interés en las artes. (Ana todavía está esperando.)
*Ana affirmed that if she got married, she would marry an intelligent man with interest in the Arts. (Ana is still waiting.)*

✔ The imperfect subjunctive is used in an if-clause (a clause introduced by **si** meaning *if*) when it refers to something considered hypothetical, contrary to fact or unlikely to happen. The verb in the main clause is in the present conditional.

Si me **avisaras** con tiempo iría a verte.
*If you told me ahead of time, I would come to see you.*

✔ The imperfect subjunctive forms of **querer** and **poder** are used to soften a request and the imperfect subjunctive forms of **deber** are used to soften a statement of obligation or advice.

**Quisiera** otra copa de vino, por favor.          **Debiéramos** guardar silencio en clase.
*I would like another glass of wine, please.*          *We should be quiet in class.*

Quizás **pudieras** ayudarme con el ensayo.
*Maybe you could help me with the essay.*

✔ To soften commands with other verbs, use the conditional.

¿Me **darías** permiso para ir?
*Would you give me permission to go?*

## 6-22 The pluperfect/past perfect subjunctive *expresses a completed action that took place in the past.*

✔ The pluperfect/past perfect subjunctive is formed by using the imperfect subjunctive of the auxiliary verb **haber** plus the **past participle** of the verb.

✔ The English equivalent is the past perfect: **had + past participle**

> hubiera
> hubieras
> hubiera
> hubiéramos      + past participle
> hubierais
> hubieran

✔ If the verb in the main clause is past (imperfect, preterite) or conditional, a subjunctive verb in the subordinate clause will be in the pluperfect subjunctive, indicating that the action in the dependent clause occurred before the action in the main clause.

Esperaba que ya **hubieras pagado** la cuenta.
*I hoped that you had already paid the bill.*

Sentí que no **hubieras llegado** a tiempo.
*I felt sorry that you had not arrived on time.*

✔ The pluperfect subjunctive is used in an if-clause (a clause introduced by **si,** meaning *if*) when it refers to a hypothetical situation that never happened. In this instance the main verb in the main clause is in the conditional perfect.

Si me **hubieses avisado** habría quemado las naves de mi imaginación.
*If you had told me, I would have burned the ships of my imagination.*

✔ After **ojalá,** the pluperfect subjunctive expresses a contrary-to-fact wish in the past.

**Ojalá** lo **hubiéramos sabido.**
*I wish we had known about it.*

CHART 10      SUBJUNCTIVE OR INDICATIVE?

| USE SUBJUNCTIVE | ← SUBJUNCTIVE OR INDICATIVE? → | USE INDICATIVE |
|:---:|---|:---:|
| ✔ | **doubt:** dudar, ser probable, **no** creer, **no** parecer, **no** pensar **que** | |
| | *but*: creer, pensar, parecer *imply certainty* | ✔ |
| ✔ | **request:** te ruego, te suplico, te pido que | |
| ✔ | **willingness:** te recomiendo, te sugiero, te aconsejo, deseo, insisto en, prefiero, te permito, quiero, exijo, te ordeno, te prohibo, necesito que | |
| ✔ | **emotion:** me apena, me alegro (de), temo, lamento, me entristece, siento mucho, me sorprende, espero **que** | |
| | *but*: *if there is no change in subject, use infinitive* | ✔ |
| ✔ | **with impersonal expressions:** es ridículo, es importante, es bueno, es malo, es necesario, es inútil, es dudoso, es extraño, es mejor, es lógico, es fácil, es una pena, es posible, es probable, es imposible, es urgente **que** | |
| | *but*: *when the subject is neither expressed nor implied, use infinitive with impersonal expressions that express certainty:* es…obvio/cierto/seguro/verdad | ✔ |
| ✔ | **with** ojalá, *and* **tal vez,** *and* **quizás,** *before the verb to express doubt or uncertainty* | |
| | *but*: **quizás** and **tal vez** *after the verb* | ✔ |
| ✔ | **in repetitive structures** *to express contradiction or submission:* Haga lo que haga no obtendré una promoción. Valga lo que valga no… | |
| ✔ | **in adverb clauses** *to relate an event or action that is indefinite. or uncertain:* para que, a fin (de) que, sin que, a menos que, a no ser que, antes (de) que, con tal (de) que, en caso (de) que | |
| ✔ | **after:** aunque, cuando, mientras, después (de) que, en cuanto, hasta que, tan pronto (como) *to introduce forthcoming events, hypothetical actions or something that has not yet occurred* | |
| | *but*: *when the aforementioned words refer to an action that has happened, is happening or habitually happens* | ✔ |
| ✔ | **in adjective clauses (unreality):** *if the antecedent is indefinite, nonexistent, hypothetical, or negative.* | |
| | *but*: *if it is definite, specific, or known to exist* | ✔ |

## CONCURRENT AND FUTURE ACTIONS

| | Main Clause → | | Subordinate Clause |
|---|---|---|---|
| present | Dudo...<br>*I doubt...* | | que el avión llegue a tiempo.<br>*that the plane will arrive on time.* |
| future | Esperaré...<br>*I will wait...* | present subjunctive | aunque tenga poco tiempo.<br>*although I have little time.* |
| present perfect | Me han aconsejado...<br>*I was advised...* | | que deje de fumar.<br>*to stop smoking.* |
| imperative | Vamos a casa...<br>*Let's go home...* | | para que cenemos juntos.<br>*so we can have dinner together.* |
| preterite | Le conté un cuento...<br>*I told her a story...* | | para que durmiera feliz.<br>*so she could sleep happily.* |
| imperfect | Siempre la acompañaba...<br>*I always accompanied her...* | imperfect subjunctive | para que no se sintiera sola.<br>*so she would not feel lonely.* |
| present conditional | Podría estudiar contigo...<br>*I could study with you...* | | si no estuviera cansado.<br>*if I were not tired.* |

## PREVIOUS ACTIONS

| | Main Clause → | | Subordinate Clause |
|---|---|---|---|
| present | Dudo...<br>*I doubt...* | | que hayas soñado conmigo.<br>*that you have dreamed of me.* |
| future | Esperaré...<br>*I will wait...* | present perfect subjunctive | a que me hayas llamado.<br>*until you have called me.* |
| imperative | Llega a las doce...<br><br>*Be here at twelve...* | | para que a las doce y media ya hayamos terminado.<br>*so that by twelve thirty we will have finished.* |
| preterite | Sentí...<br>*I felt sorry...* | | que hubieras llegado atrasada.<br>*that you had arrived late.* |
| imperfect | Esperaba...<br>*I expected...* | pluperfect/ past perfect subjunctive | que me hubieses despertado antes.<br>*that you would have woken me earlier.* |
| conditional perfect | Ella habría podido desayunar...<br>*She would have had breakfast...* | | si no se hubiera levantado tan tarde.<br>*if she hadn't got up so late.* |

CHART 12

| SUBJECT | INFINITIVE | PRESENT | | PRETERITE | | IMPERFECT | |
|---|---|---|---|---|---|---|---|
| **pronoun** | | infinitive minus | plus | infinitive minus | plus | infinitive minus | plus |
| yo | amar | -ar | -o | -ar | -é | -ar | -aba |
| tú | | | -as | | -aste | | -abas |
| usted/él/ella | | | -a | | -ó | | -aba |
| nosotros(as) | | | -amos | | -amos | | -ábamos |
| vosotros(as) | | | -áis | | -asteis | | -abais |
| ustedes/ellos(as) | | | -an | | -aron | | -aban |
| yo | comer | -er | -o | -er | -í | -er | -ía |
| tú | | | -es | | -iste | | -ías |
| usted/él/ella | | | -e | | -ió | | -ía |
| nosotros(as) | | | -emos | | -imos | | -íamos |
| vosotros(as) | | | -éis | | -isteis | | -íais |
| ustedes/ellos(as) | | | -en | | -ieron | | -ían |
| yo | partir | -ir | -o | -ir | -í | -ir | -ía |
| tú | | | -es | | -iste | | -ías |
| usted/él/ella | | | -e | | -ió | | -ía |
| nosotros(as) | | | -imos | | -imos | | -íamos |
| vosotros(as) | | | -ís | | -isteis | | -íais |
| ustedes/ellos(as) | | | -en | | -ieron | | -ían |

CHART 12 (CONT.) PATTERNS OF CONJUGATION OF -AR, -ER, -IR REGULAR VERBS

| SUBJECT | INFINITIVE | FUTURE | | CONDITIONAL | | SUBJUNCTIVE | |
|---------|-----------|--------|--|-------------|--|-------------|--|
| **pronoun** | | infinitive | plus | infinitive | plus | **yo-form,** present indicative | plus |
| yo | amar | infinitive | -é | infinitive | -ía | **am**o – o | -e |
| tú | | | -ás | | -ías | | -es |
| usted/él/ella | | | -á | | -ía | | -e |
| nosotros(as) | | | -emos | | -íamos | | -emos |
| vosotros(as) | | | -éis | | -íais | | -eis |
| ustedes/ellos(as) | | | -án | | -ían | | -en |
| yo | comer | infin. | -é | infinitive | -ía | **com**o – o | -a |
| tú | | | -ás | | -ías | | -as |
| usted/él/ella | | | -á | | -ía | | -a |
| nosotros(as) | | | -emos | | -íasmos | | -amos |
| vosotros(as) | | | -éis | | -íasis | | -áis |
| ustedes/ellos(as) | | | -án | | -ían | | -an |
| yo | partir | | -é | infinitive | -ía | **part**o – o | -a |
| tú | | | -ás | | -ías | | -as |
| usted/él/ella | | | -á | | -ía | | -a |
| nosotros(as) | | | -emos | | -íamos | | -amos |
| vosotros(as) | | | -éis | | -íais | | -áis |
| ustedes/ellos(as) | | | -án | | -ían | | -an |

**6-23 The imperative** *is a mood that expresses commands, requests, or directions.*

✔ The imperative is formed by adding **-e** or **-a** to the stem of the first-person singular of the present indicative.

**6-23a Formal commands** *(usted)* of *-ar* verbs add *-e* to the stem.

| comprar | stem | + | e |
|---------|------|---|---|
| compro → | compr → | | compre |

*Note:* **estar** and **dar** have irregular formal commands: **esté-estén / dé-den**

**6-23b Formal commands** of *-er* and *-ir* verbs add *-a* to the stem.

| **comer** | stem | + | a |
|-----------|------|---|---|
| como → | com → | | coma |

*Note:* **ser, saber** and **ir** have irregular formal commands

| sea-sean | sepa-sepan | vaya-vayan |
|----------|------------|------------|

✔ If a verb stem is irregular in the **yo** *(I)* form of the present tense, this irregularity carries over to the command form.

| decir | → | diga | hacer | → | haga |
|-------|---|------|-------|---|------|
| oír | → | oiga | poner | → | ponga |
| salir | → | salga | tener | → | tenga |
| ver | → | vea | venir | → | venga |

**6-23c Plural commands**

✔ The command for **ustedes** is formed by adding **-n** to the **usted** command form.

| coma | → | coma**n** | compre→ | compre**n** |
|------|---|-----------|---------|-------------|

✔ The command form of **nosotros** is the same as the first-person plural in the present subjunctive.*

comamos = comamos   *let's eat*

*The exception is **ir. Vamos** is the positive command; **no vayamos** is used for the negative command.

✔ Note that the command forms for the **usted(es)** and **nosotros(as)** verb forms are identical to the corresponding present subjunctive forms.

✔ The negative is formed by placing **no** before the verb in the command form.

| coma/n | → | **no** coma/n |
|--------|---|---------------|
| comamos | → | **no** comamos |

✔ The use of **usted** or **ustedes** is optional. These pronouns are used to give emphasis or to clarify.

✔ In commands, **usted** or **ustedes** normally follows the verb.

> *Pase **usted**.*          Sigan **ustedes**.

✔ In affirmative commands, object pronouns and reflexive pronouns must follow the command form and be attached to it.

> ¡Béban**la**!               ¡Acosté**monos**!
> *Drink it!*                 *Let's go to bed!*

✔ In negative commands, object pronouns and reflexive pronouns precede the verb but they are not attached to it.

> ¡No **la** beban!           ¡No **nos** acostemos!
> *Do not drink it!*          *Let's not go to bed!*

✔ When the first-person plural command is used with a reflexive verb or the indirect object pronoun **se**, the final **s** of the verb is dropped before adding **nos** or **se**.

> Es mejor que nos vistamos.      ¡Vistámonos!
> *It is better that we get dressed.*   *Let's get dressed!*

> ¡Pidámosle el libro!            ¡Pidámoselo!
> *Let's ask him for the book!*   *Let's ask for it!*

**6-23d Informal commands (tú)** are used to give instructions or commands to people you address with the informal *you*. This includes close friends, children, etc.

✔ The affirmative informal (**tú**) command for regular verbs is identical to the third-person singular form of the present indicative.

| infinitive | | present indicative | | command (tú) |
|---|---|---|---|---|
| pensar | → | él piensa | → | **piensa** |
| vender | → | él vende | → | **vende** |
| dormir | → | él duerme | → | **duerme** |

**6-23e Irregular affirmative informal commands**

| decir | → | di | hacer | → | haz |
|---|---|---|---|---|---|
| ir | → | ve* | poner | → | pon |
| salir | → | sal | ser | → | sé |
| tener | → | ten | venir | → | ven |

*Note:* **ir** and **ver** have the same affirmative informal command: **ve**

## 6–23f Negative informal commands

✔ The negative informal command for regular verbs is identical to the second-person singular form of the present subjunctive.

| infinitive | | present subjunctive | | negative informal command *(tú)* |
|---|---|---|---|---|
| tomar | → | que tú tomes | → | **no tomes** |
| volver | → | que tú vuelvas | → | **no vuelvas** |
| dormir | → | que tú duermas | → | **no duermas** |
| ir | → | que tú vayas | → | **no vayas** |

✔ In negative commands, object pronouns and reflexive pronouns precede the verb and are not attached to it.

¡Bébela!      ¡No **la** bebas!
*Drink it!*      *Don't drink it!*

✔ When two object pronouns (direct and indirect) are used, the indirect pronoun precedes the direct object pronoun.

¡**Tómate** la sopa!      ¡No **te la** tomes!
*Drink your soup!*      *Don't drink it!*

¡Dímelo!      ¡No **me lo** digas!
*Tell it to me!*      *Don't tell it to me!*

---

| CHART 13 | COMPARISON OF VERB TENSES IN SPANISH AND ENGLISH |
|---|---|

| HABLAR | (TO SPEAK) |
|---|---|
| **PRESENTE**<br>hablo | **PRESENT**<br>*I speak* |
| **PRESENTE PROGRESIVO**<br>**presente de *estar* + participio presente**<br>estoy hablando | **PRESENT PROGRESSIVE**<br>**present of *to be* + -ing form**<br>*I am speaking* |
| **PRETÉRITO PERFECTO**<br>**presente de *haber* + participio pasado**<br>he hablado | **PRESENT PERFECT**<br>***have/has* + past participle**<br>*I have spoken* |
| **PRETÉRITO INDEFINIDO**<br>hablé | **PAST OR PRETERITE**<br>*I spoke* |
| **PASADO PROGRESIVO**<br>**imperfecto de *estar* + participio presente**<br>estaba hablando | **PAST PROGRESSIVE**<br>***was/were* + -ing form**<br>*I was speaking* |
| **PRETÉRITO ANTERIOR**<br>**Pretérito indefinido de *haber* + participio pasado**<br>hube hablado | **PAST PERFECT**<br>***had* + past participle**<br>*I had spoken* |

CHART 13 (CONT.) COMPARISON OF VERB TENSES IN SPANISH AND ENGLISH

| HABLAR | (TO SPEAK) |
|---|---|
| **IMPERFECTO**<br>hablaba | **IMPERFECT**<br>*I used to speak* |
| **PLUSCUAMPERFECTO**<br>Imperfecto de *haber* + participio pasado<br>había hablado | **PLUPERFECT**<br>**Corresponds to the past perfect**<br>*had* + past participle<br>*I had spoken* |
| **FUTURO**<br>hablaré | **FUTURE**<br>*I will (shall) speak* |
| **FUTURO INMEDIATO**<br>presente de *ir* + *a* + infinitivo<br>Voy a hablar | **NEAR FUTURE**<br>*to be going* + infinitive<br>*I'm going to speak* |
| **FUTURO PERFECTO**<br>futuro de *haber* + participio pasado<br>habré hablado | **FUTURE PERFECT**<br>*will/shall have* + past participle<br>*I will have spoken* |
| **FUTURO PROGRESIVO**<br>habré estado + participio presente<br>habré estado hablando | **FUTURE PROGRESSIVE**<br>*will/shall have been* + present participle<br>*I will have been speaking* |
| **CONDICIONAL: PRESENTE**<br>infinitivo + terminaciones<br>*-ía/-ías/-ía /-íamos/-íais/-ían*<br>hablaría | **CONDITIONAL: PRESENT**<br>*would* + base form<br>*would speak* |
| **CONDICIONAL: PASADO**<br>condicional presente de<br>*haber* + participio pasado<br>habría hablado | **CONDITIONAL: PERFECT**<br>*would* + *have* + past participle<br>*would have spoken* |
| **SUBJUNTIVO: PRESENTE**<br>elimine la *-o* de la primera persona singular<br>del presente del indicativo + las terminaciones<br>-ar: *-e/-es/-e / -emos/-éis/-en*<br>-er/-ir: *-a/-as/-a / -amos/-áis/-an*<br>que yo hable | **SUBJUNCTIVE: PRESENT**<br>present minus -s of the third-person singular:<br>base form of the verb<br>*that I speak* |
| **SUBJUNTIVO: IMPERFECTO**<br>tercera persona plural del pretérito indefinido<br>menos *-ron* + terminaciones<br>*-ra/-ras/-ra / -ramos/-rais/-ran*<br>hablara | **SUBJUNCTIVE: IMPERFECT**<br>corresponds to past tense indicative<br>*that I spoke* |
| **SUBJUNTIVO: PRETÉRITO PERFECTO**<br>presente del subjuntivo de<br>*haber* + participio pasado<br>haya hablado | **SUBJUNCTIVE: PRESENT PERFECT**<br>corresponds to present perfect indicative<br>*that I have spoken* |

CHART 13 (CONT.) COMPARISON OF VERB TENSES IN SPANISH AND ENGLISH

| HABLAR | (TO SPEAK) |
|---|---|
| SUBJUNTIVO: PLUSCUAMPERFECTO<br>Pluperfect or Past perfect<br>imperfecto del subjuntivo de *haber* + participio pasado<br>hubiera hablado | SUBJUNCTIVE: PAST PERFECT<br>corresponds to past perfect indicative<br>*that I had spoken* |
| IMPERATIVO: FORMAL<br>raíz de la primera persona singular<br>del presente del indicativo<br>+*e* [verbos -ar]<br>+*a* [verbos -er/ir]<br>¡Hable! | IMPERATIVE<br>infinitive minus *to*<br><br><br><br>*Speak!* |
| IMPERATIVO: INFORMAL afirmativo es igual a<br>la 3a persona singular del presente indicativo<br>¡Habla!<br>negativo es igual a la 2a persona singular<br>del presente subjuntivo<br>¡No hables! | *Speak!*<br><br>*Don't speak!* |

## 6-24 Ser and estar

Spanish possesses two verbs meaning **to be**. They are not interchangeable.

**Ser** generally denotes characteristics or qualities that cannot be changed and is used to define or to tell who or what the subject is.

**Estar** is used to describe conditions that indicate a change or deviation from what is normal for the person or thing being described, or to indicate locations, whether permanent or temporary.

### 6-24a  ser

**singular**

| yo | soy | *I am* |
|---|---|---|
| tú | eres | *you are (informal)* |
| usted/él/ella | es | *you are (formal)/he/she is* |

**plural**

| nosotros(as) | somos | *we are* |
|---|---|---|
| vosotros(as) | sois | *you are (informal)* |
| ustedes/ellos(as) | son | *you are (formal)/they are* |

✔ **Ser** is used with adjectives to describe physical characteristics.

El árbol **es** grande.
*The tree is tall.*

Pedro **es** bajo.
*Pedro is short.*

✔ **Ser** is used with adjectives to describe personality traits and inherent characteristics.

Tu hermano **es** simpático.
*Your brother is nice.*

Juan **es** delgado.
*Juan is thin.*

El auto **es** cómodo.
*The car is comfortable.*

✔ **Ser** is used to identify people or things.

Yo **soy** estudiante de español y éstos **son** mis libros de texto.
*I am a student of Spanish and these are my textbooks.*

La doctora Mateluna **es** profesora.
*Dr. Mateluna is a professor.*

✔ **Ser** is used to ask for identification, to discuss what a person is like, or to talk about a person's profession.

¿Quién **es**?
*Who is it?*

**Es** Pablo.
*It is Pablo.*

¿Cómo **es**?
*How is he? (What is he like?)*

**Es** buena persona.
*He is a good person.*

¿Qué **es**?
*What is he?*

**Es** escritor
*He is a writer.*

✔ **Ser** is used to express nationality.

**Soy** norteamericano(a).
*I am North American.*

**Somos** españoles/españolas.
*We are Spanish.*

✔ **Ser** plus the preposition **de** and the name of a country, city, or place is used to express origin, (to be from).

**Somos** de Nueva York.
*We are from New York.*

**Soy** de Guadalajara.
*I am from Guadalajara.*

✔ **Ser** is used to tell what materials things are made of.

La mecedora **es** de madera.
*The rocking chair is made of wood.*

Las sillas **son** de plástico.
*The chairs are plastic.*

✔ **Ser** is used to tell time.

¡Ya **son** las dos!
*It is already two!*

**Es** la una y cinco.
*It is five minutes after one.*

✔ **Ser** is used to discuss time in a general way.

Es la hora de comer.
*It is time to eat.*

Es tarde.
*It is late.*

✔ **Ser** is used to talk about days of the week.

¿Qué día **es** hoy?
*What day is it?*

Hoy **es** miércoles.
*It is Wednesday.*

✔ **Ser** is used to tell dates.

¿Qué fecha **es** hoy?
*What is today's date?*

Hoy **es** 25 de diciembre.
*Today is December 25th.*

✔ **Ser** is used to indicate where an event takes place.

El concierto **es** en el teatro municipal
*The concert is in the Municipal Theater.*

La fiesta **es** en casa de Juana.
*The party is at Juana's house.*

✔ The imperfect forms of **ser** (**era** o **eran**), indicate the time an action took place.

**Era** la una cuando ocurrió el accidente.
*It was one o'clock when the accident took place.*

**Eran** las diez cuando Pedro me llamó.
*It was ten o'clock when Pedro called me.*

✔ **Ser** is used to form impersonal expressions and to express generalizations, opinions, and ideas that are generally held to be true.

Es una lástima...
*It is a pity/shame . . .*

Es importante...
*It is important . . .*

Es evidente...
*It is evident . . .*

Es necesario practicar deportes todos los días.
*It is necessary to practice a sport every day.*

Es importante estudiar español.
*It is important to study Spanish.*

✔ **Ser** is used to show possession.

Es mi casa.
*It is my house.*

Son mis hijos.
*They are my children.*

El auto **es** de María.
*The car is María's.*

✔ **Ser** combined with **para,** tells for whom or what something is intended.

Las cartas **son** para mi hermano.
*The letters are for my brother.*

¿Para qué **es** este libro?
*What is this book for?*

Es para aprender español.
*It is for learning Spanish.*

✔ Mathematical equations require **ser.**

Uno más dos **son** tres.
*One plus two is three.*

Diez menos nueve **es** uno.
*Ten minus nine is one.*

✔ Passive constructions use the present or the preterite of **ser: (es** or **son, fue** or **fueron) + the past participle.**

Los periódicos **son** entregados por Elmer.
*The newspapers are delivered by Elmer.*

El libro **fue** escrito por García Márquez.
*The book was written by García Márquez.*

✔ **Ser** appears before an infinitive.

Querer **es** poder.
*Where there's a will there's a way.*

Lo importante **es** soñar.
*What matters is to dream.*

## 6–24b  estar

### singular

| yo | estoy | *I am* |
|---|---|---|
| tú | estás | *you are (informal, singular)* |
| usted/él/ella | está | *you are (formal, singular)/he/she is* |

### plural

| nosotros(as) | estamos | *we are* |
|---|---|---|
| vosotros(as) | estáis | *you are (informal plural)* |
| ustedes/ellos(as) | están | *you are (formal plural)/they are* |

✔ **Estar** is used with adjectives to describe physical or emotional states or the condition of someone or something at a given moment.

| ¿Cómo **está** usted? | *How are you doing?* |
|---|---|
| **Estoy** bien, gracias. | *I'm fine, thank you.* |
| **Estoy** triste. | *I'm sad.* |
| **Estoy** enfermo. | *I'm sick.* |
| **Estoy** cansado.* | *I'm tired.* |
| **Estoy** preocupado, Juan **está** muy **delgado.** | *I'm worried; Juan is exceedingly thin.* |
| El auto **está** sucio. | *The car is dirty.* |
| **Está** muerto. * | *He is dead.* (because being dead has the religious connotation of temporality.) |

*The adjectives **cansado, contento,** and **muerto** are always used with **estar.**

✔ **Estar** is used with adjectives to describe behavior at a particular moment.

Juan, **estás** insoportable.
*Juan, you are (being) unbearable.*

Hoy **están** muy **perezosos**.
*You are very lazy today.*

✔ **Estar** is used with adjectives to describe weather conditions at a particular moment.

**Está** nublado.
*It is cloudy.*

**Está** soleado.
*It is sunny.*

✔ **Estar** is used with the past participle to describe conditions or states of being. When past participles function as adjectives, they must agree in gender and number with their subject.

La copa **está rota**.
*The glass is broken.*

Es fin de semestre y **estamos cansados**.
*It is the end of the semester and we are tired.*

La calefacción **estaba desconectada** cuando comenzó a nevar.
*The heating was off when it started to snow.*

✔ **Estar** indicates the location of someone or something in space or time.

Juan **está** en la universidad.
*Juan is at the university.*

**Estamos** en primavera.
*It is spring.*

La casa **está** cerca de la playa.
*The house is near the beach.*

**Estamos** en enero.
*It is January.*

✔ **Estar** is used to form the **progressive tense**.

**estar + the present participle***

María **está** comiendo tacos.
*María is eating tacos.*

¿Qué **estás haciendo**?
*What are you doing?*

**Está** lloviendo mucho.
*It is raining a lot.*

**Estoy hablando** por teléfono.
*I am talking on the phone.*

*The present participle of Spanish verbs is formed by adding the suffix **-ando** to the stem of **-ar** verbs and the suffix **-iendo** to the stem of **-er** and **-ir** verbs. It corresponds to the *-ing* form in English.

Estoy estudi-**ando** español.
*I am study**ing** Spanish.*

Estoy viv-**iendo** en New York.
*I am liv**ing** in New York.*

Estoy com-**iendo** tacos.
*I am eat**ing** tacos.*

✔ Verbs that are **stem-changing -ir verbs** (o → u, and e → i) in the third-person preterite, will show the same change in the present participle.

| | | |
|---|---|---|
| poder | → | pu**d**iendo |
| dormir | → | du**rm**iendo |
| preferir | → | prefi**r**iendo |
| pedir | → | pi**d**iendo |

✔ When the stem of an **-er** or **-ir** verb ends in a vowel, the **i** changes to **y**.

| iendo | → | yendo |
|---|---|---|
| leer | → | leyendo |
| traer | → | trayendo |
| caer | → | cayendo |
| ir | → | yendo |

✔ The imperfect of **estar + present participle,** or the **past progressive,** describes what someone was doing at a given moment. The past progressive emphasizes the ongoing nature of the action.

Corría *(imperfect)* cuando llamaste.
*I was running when you called.*

**Estábamos corriendo** cuando llamaste.
*We were running when you called.*

✔ **Estar** is used with a number of fixed expressions.

| | |
|---|---|
| (no) **estar** bien/mal | *to be well/bad* |
| (no) **estar** claro | *to be clear* |
| (no) **estar** de vacaciones | *to be on vacation* |
| (no) **estar** de acuerdo | *to agree* |
| (no) **estar** de viaje | *to be traveling* |
| (no) **estar** de compras | *to do shopping* |
| (no) **estar** de luto | *to be in mourning* |
| (no) **estar** de buen/mal humor | *to be in a good/bad mood* |
| (no) **estar** de buenas/malas | *to be in a good/bad mood* |

## 6-24c ser vs. estar

✔ **Ser** is used to tell time: hour, day, and date.

✔ **Estar** is never used to tell time: hour, day, or date.

✔ **Ser** asks or tells **¿qué?** *(what?)* or **¿quién?** *(who?)* with adjectives.

✔ Used with **ser,** the adjective denotes essential qualities or basic characteristics.

✔ Age and financial position (**joven, viejo(a), rico(a), pobre**) are considered characteristics.

| | |
|---|---|
| Juan **es** pálido. | *Juan is pale.* |
| La película **es** interesante. | *The movie is interesting.* |
| Inés **es** joven. | *Inés is young.* |

✔ With **estar**, the adjective denotes a temporary condition. In general when *to be* implies *looks like, tastes like, feels like* or *appears like*, **estar** is used.

Tras el accidente Juan **está** pálido.
*After the accident Juan looks pale.*

Los alumnos **están** felices.
*The students are happy.*

✔ The choice between **ser + adjective** or **estar + adjective** emphasizes the difference between the norm and variation from the norm.

Juan **es** pálido, pero hoy **está** más pálido que de costumbre.
*Juan is pale, but today he looks paler than usual.*

### 6-24d  Adjectives with different meanings depending on whether they are used with *ser* or *estar*

| ser | estar |
|---|---|
| Juan **es** listo. | Juan **está** listo |
| *Juan is smart.* | *Juan is ready.* |
| El niño **es** vivo. | El niño **está** vivo. |
| *The child is smart.* | *The child is alive.* |
| Ella **es** mala. | Ella **está** mala. |
| *She is bad. (evil)* | *She is sick.* |
| La uva **es** verde. | La uva **está** verde. |
| *The grape is green.* | *The grape is unripe.* |
| Mi padre **es** rico. | El pastel **está** rico. |
| *My father is rich.* | *The cake is delicious.* |

### 6-24e  Estar vs. haber

✔ To express *there is* and *there are*, Spanish uses the verb **haber** in the impersonal form **hay**.

**Hay varios** niños en el parque.
*There are several kids in the park.*

**Hay uno** que es más grande que los otros.
*There is one who is bigger than the others.*

✔ To express *there was* or *there were*, use **hubo** or **había**.

Ayer **hubo** una fiesta en casa de Juan.
*Yesterday there was a party at Juan's house.*

**Había** mucha gente mirando el desfile.
*There were many people watching the parade.*

✔ **Hay** can be used in any tense or mood; it will always be invariable.

Espero que **haya** suficientes frutas para la ensalada.
*I hope there will be enough fruit for the salad.*

## 6-25 Saber vs. conocer

✔ Both verbs mean **to know,** but they represent two different kinds of knowledge and they are not interchangeable.

| saber | conocer |
|-------|---------|
| sé | conozco |
| sabes | conoces |
| sabe | conoce |
| sabemos | conocemos |
| sabéis | conocéis |
| saben | conocen |

**6-25a  Saber** means to know facts or information, to know thoroughly, or by heart.

Sé la lección al dedillo.
*I know the lesson by heart.*

✔ **Saber** may be followed by a noun or pronoun representing something that has been learned.

Pepita y sus amigos **saben** la canción.
*Pepita and her friends know the song by heart.*

✔ In questions, **saber** is used to ask for information.

¿*Sabes* dónde está la biblioteca?           ¿**Sabes** quién escribió *Don Quijote*?
*Do you know where the library is?*           *Do you know who wrote Don Quijote?*

¿Sabes dónde, cuándo, cómo, qué, por qué, quién, con quién, a quién, cuánto, cuál...?
*Do you know where, when, how, what, why, who, with whom, to whom, how much/many, which one...?*

✔ **Saber** is usually followed by a clause or an infinitive.

**Sabemos** quién fue el ganador.
*We know who the winner was.*

✔ When followed by an infinitive, **saber** means *to know how to do something.*

Alejandro y Melina **saben** tocar el piano.
*Alejandro and Melina know how to play the piano.*

Ellos **saben** hablar español, francés e inglés.
*They know how to speak Spanish, French, and English.*

✔ In the preterite, **saber** means *to know, to learn, to find out about.*

¿**Supiste** que María se casó ayer?
*Did you know that María got married yesterday?*

**6-25b Conocer** means *to know* as the result of direct experience.

✔ **Conocer** is only used with a noun or pronoun.

✔ **Conocer** cannot be followed by an infinitive nor a clause.

✔ **Conocer** followed by the preposition **a + person** means *to know* in the sense of *to be acquainted with someone.*

| | |
|---|---|
| **¿Conoces** a Juan Carlos? | **¿Conoces** *a sus padres?* |
| *Do you know Juan Carlos?* | *Do you know his/her parents?* |

**Conozco** al nuevo profesor.
*I know the new professor.*

✔ Followed directly by a noun referring to a thing or place, **conocer** means *to be familiar with.*

Juan no **conoce** Madrid pero **conoce** Barcelona.
*Juan does not know Madrid, but he knows Barcelona.*

**¿Conoces** un buen restaurante francés? No, pero **conozco** un **excelente** restaurante mexicano.
*Do you know a good French restaurant? No, but I know an excellent Mexican restaurant.*

✔ In the preterite, **conocer** means *to meet for the first time.*

En Europa **conocí** a mi esposa.
*In Europe I met my wife.*

✔ Notice the difference between the way **saber** and **conocer** are used in the following example.

No **conozco** a la autora de *La casa de los espíritus* personalmente, pero **sé** que se llama Isabel Allende.
*I don't know the author of* La casa de los espíritus *personally, but I know that she is Isabel Allende.*

## 6-26 Saber/poder

✔ Note the distinction between **saber** and **poder**, both of which sometimes mean *can* in English.

✔ **Poder** indicate that you are able to do something.

✔ To indicates mental ability, **saber** is used.

| | |
|---|---|
| **¿Sabe** usted leer? | Sí, **sé** leer. |
| *Do you know how to read?* | *Yes, I know.* |

✔ If the verb expresses physical ability, **poder** is used.

| | |
|---|---|
| **¿Puede** usted leerme esta carta? | Lo siento, no **puedo**, no tengo mis lentes. |
| *Can you read me this letter?* | *I'm sorry, I cannot, I don't have my glasses with me.* |
| **¿Puede** usted bailar? | No **puedo**, tengo la pierna quebrada. |
| *Can you (are you able to) dance?* | *I cannot; my leg is broken.* |

|  | poder *(to be able to, can)* singular | saber *(to know)* singular |
|---|---|---|
| yo | puedo | sé |
| tú | puedes | sabes |
| usted/él/ella | puede | sabe |
|  | **plural** | **plural** |
| nosotros(as) | podemos | sabemos |
| vosotros(as) | podéis | sabéis |
| ustedes/ellos(as) | pueden | saben |

## 6-27 Idiomatic expressions with verbs

### 6-27a *Hacer* with expressions of time and weather

**hacer + expressions of time**

✔ **Hace + period of time + que + present tense verb** is used to express an action that began in the past and is still going on.

**Hace tres años que vivo** en esta ciudad.
*I have been living in this city for three years.*

✔ **Hace + period of time + que + preterite tense verb** is used to express how long ago an action took place.

Hace cinco años que se graduó.
*He graduated five years ago.*

✔ **Hacía + period of time + que + the imperfect tense** is used to refer to an action that started in the past and was still going on when another action took place.

**Hacía** dos años que **vivía** en Madrid cuando le ofrecieron un puesto en Barcelona.
*He had been living in Madrid for two years when he was offered a job in Barcelona.*

✔ If the clause normally introduced by **que** occurs before the clause using **hacer, que** is omitted.

Hace cinco años que se graduó. Se graduó hace cinco años.
*He/She graduated five years ago.*

✔ To ask questions using **hacer + expressions of time,** use the following structure:

**Cuánto + period of time + hace (hacía) + que +verb**

**¿Cuántas semanas hace que tomaste** el examen?
*How many weeks has it been since you took the exam?*

**¿Cuánto tiempo hacía que no venías** a vernos?
*How long has it been since you visited us?*

✔ There are other expressions equivalent to **¿cuánto tiempo…?**. **¿Cuándo?** and **¿desde cuándo?** are also used to ask questions.

**¿Cuándo** empezaste? Hace diez minutos.
*When did you begin? Ten minutes ago.*

**¿Desde cuándo** trabajas aquí? Desde hace un año.
*Since when have you been working here? I've been working here for a year.*

**hacer + weather expressions**

✔ Use **hace + weather expressions** to express most weather conditions.

| | |
|---|---|
| ¡Qué frío hace! | *How cold it is!* |
| ¡Qué calor hace! | *How hot it is!* |
| ¿Qué tiempo hace? | *What is the weather like?* |
| Hace (mucho) frío. | *It is (very) cold.* |
| Hace (mucho) calor. | *It is (very) hot.* |
| Hace (mucho) viento. | *It is (very) windy.* |
| Hace (mucho) sol | *It is (very) sunny.* |

✔ Because **frío, calor, viento,** and **sol** are nouns, **mucho** (not **muy**) is used to express *very,* but you say

Hace (muy) mal tiempo.          Hace (muy) buen tiempo.
*It is (very) stormy.*               *It is (very) nice out.*

**6-27b Idiomatic expressions with *tener***

a form of **tener + a noun**

✔ To modify the nouns used in the following idiomatic expressions, use an adjective: **mucho(a), poco(a).** Never use **muy.**

| | | |
|---|---|---|
| | hambre | celos |
| | *hungry* | *jealous* |
| | sed | prisa |
| | *thirsty* | *in a hurry* |
| **tener** | frío | suerte |
| *(to be)* | *cold* | *lucky* |
| | calor | razón |
| | *hot* | *right* |
| | sueño | cuidado |
| | *sleepy* | *careful* |
| | miedo | éxito |
| | *afraid* | *successful* |

tener... años
*to be . . . years old*

Tengo veinte años.
*I am twenty years old.*

**tener ganas de + infinitive** *to feel like* . . . (literally *to have the desire to*)

María y yo tenemos ganas de ir al cine.
*María and I feel like going to the movies.*

| | |
|---|---|
| tener dolor de... <br> *to have pain* | tener fiebre* <br> *to have a fever* |
| Tengo dolor de cabeza. <br> *I have a headache.* | Tengo **mucha** fiebre*. <br> *I have a high fever.* |

**\*Fiebre, razón, hambre, sed,** and **suerte** are feminine.

✔ **Tener que + infinitive** *(to have to)*

Tengo que estudiar para el examen.
*I have to study for the exam.*

## 6-27c Idiomatic expressions with *estar*

✔ Expressions with **estar** are used to express conditions or feelings. To modify the adjective, use the adverb **muy.** Never use **mucho(a).**

A form of **estar + an adjective**

| | |
|---|---|
| **estoy** cansado(a) <br> *I am tired* | Estoy **muy** cansada. <br> *I'm very tired.* |

The following adjectives are generally used with **estar** to express conditions or feelings:

| | | | |
|---|---|---|---|
| contento(a) <br> *happy* | ocupado(a) <br> *busy* | alegre <br> *happy* | seguro(a) <br> *sure* |
| triste <br> *sad* | preocupado(a) <br> *worried* | listo(a) <br> *ready* | vivo(a) <br> *alive* |
| aburrido(a) <br> *bored* | nervioso(a) <br> *nervous* | loco(a) <br> *crazy* | muerto(a) <br> *dead* |

# CHAPTER 7

## *Prepositions*

**PREPOSITIONS** are invariable connecting words placed before a substantive that indicate the relation of that substantive to the verb, an adjective, or another substantive.

✔ **of place:** sobre, detrás de

✔ **of time:** antes de, después de

✔ **of purpose:** para

✔ **of possession:** de

✔ **of manner:** con

Le escribí a mi mamá **antes de** ir al cine.
*I wrote my mother before going to the movies.*

Lo hice **contra** viento y marea.
*I did it against all the odds.*

¡Cuán **lejos de** mí está el mar!
*How far from me is the sea!*

**Tras** la humilde tapa se esconde una obra maestra.
*Behind the humble cover, there is a masterpiece.*

De regreso **de** Santiago pasé **por** Lo Miranda.
*Returning from Santiago, I passed by Lo Miranda.*

¿Quién llamó **a** la puerta?
*Who knocked at the door?*

✔ The preposition **con** (*with*) has special forms for the first- and second-person singular: **conmigo, contigo.**

Puedes ir **conmigo** al restaurante.
*You can come to the restaurant with me.*

**Contigo** seré feliz.
*I will be happy with you.*

CHART 14          PREPOSITIONS

| SIMPLE PREPOSITIONS | | | | |
|---|---|---|---|---|
| a<br>*to, at* | ante<br>*before* | bajo<br>*under* | cabe, cabe decir<br>*it is worth* | con<br>*with* |
| contra<br>*against* | de<br>*of, about, from* | desde<br>*from, since* | en<br>*in, on, at* | entre<br>*between* |
| hacia<br>*toward* | hasta<br>*until* | para<br>*for, in order to* | por<br>*in, on, at* | según<br>*according to* |
| sin<br>*without* | sobre<br>*about, on, above* | tras<br>*behind* | | |

| COMPOUND PREPOSITIONS | | | | |
|---|---|---|---|---|
| al lado de<br>*next to, beside* | antes de<br>*before* | cerca de<br>*close to, near* | debajo de<br>*below, under* | delante de<br>*in front of* |
| dentro de<br>*inside* | desde que<br>*since* | después de<br>*after* | detrás de<br>*behind* | encima de<br>*above, on top of* |
| enfrente de<br>*in front of* | entre sí<br>*among* | en vez de<br>*instead of* | fuera de<br>*of outside* | lejos de<br>*far from* |

## 7-1 The preposition *a*

✔ The preposition a is used to indicate a movement toward a place or a final destination.

Mañana iremos **a** Nueva York.
*Tomorrow we will go to New York.*

Se fueron **a** otro país.
*They left for another country.*

*but* **hasta** can substitute for **a** between a verb of movement and a noun to show final destination.

El camino llega **hasta** la cima.
*The road leads to the top.*

✔ A is used before a noun expressing length, distance or content.

El hospital queda **a** 10 millas de aquí.
*The hospital is ten miles from here.*

*but* **hacia** can replace **a** before certain nouns expressing movement toward a direction.

Tienes que girar **hacia** la izquierda en el semáforo.
*You must make a left at the traffic light.*

✔ **A** is used before nouns expressing time or age.

La cita es **a** las ocho.
*The appointment is at eight.*

Dio su primer recital de piano a los cuatro años.
*He gave his first piano recital at the age of four.*

## 7-1a   The personal *a*

✔ The personal **a** is used to introduce direct objects when they refer to specific people, groups of people, or pets.

Conocí **a** los hijos de María.
*I met María's children.*

✘ When the direct object is unidentified, hypothetical, a thing, or a place, the **personal a** is usually omitted.

Conocí unos niños en el parque.
*I met a few kids in the park.*

Busco la calle Moneda.
*I am looking for Moneda Street.*

✔ The **personal a** is used with persons, when the direct object is **quien(es)** or an indefinite or negative word like **alguien**, **alguna**, **nadie**, **ningún**, etc.

Voy a visitar a mis padres.
*I'm going to visit my parents.*

No quiero ver **a** nadie.
*I don't want to see anybody.*

¿A quién llamaste?
*Whom did you call?*

## 7-1b   Verbs requiring the preposition *a*

✔ Some verbs require the preposition **a** when followed by an infinitive.

| | | |
|---|---|---|
| aprender (a) *to learn* | comenzar *to begin* | decidirse *to decide* |
| detenerse *to stop* | enseñar *to teach* | ir *to go* |

Ya aprendí **a** manejar.
*I already learned to drive.*

✔ Some verbs require the preposition **a** when followed by a noun.

| asistir | entrar | llamar |
|---------|--------|--------|
| *to attend* | *to enter* | *to call* |

Juana entró **a** la casa.
*Juana entered the house.*

✔ Some verbs require the preposition **a** when followed by a noun or an infinitive.

| ayudar | correr | invitar |
|--------|--------|---------|
| *to help* | *to run* | *to invite* |

| llegar | salir | volver |
|--------|-------|--------|
| *to arrive* | *to leave* | *to return* |

Luis me invitó **a** bailar/baile.
*Luis invited me to dance/the dance.*

Some verbs use **a** only to introduce nouns referring to people, pets, personnified objects, quien(es), or indefinite or negative words such as **alguien, alguna, nadie, ningún,** etc.

| amar | buscar | conocer |
|------|--------|---------|
| *to love* | *to look for* | *to know* |

| encontrar | visitar |
|-----------|---------|
| *to meet* | *to visit* |

Conozco **a** Pedro.
*I know Pedro.*

## 7-2 The preposition *en*

✔ The **preposition en** is used after a verb to indicate location without the idea of movement.

Está **en** casa.                     Vive **en** Roma.
*He is at home.*                      *He lives in Rome.*

✔ **En** is used to indicate the place where an action or event takes place.

El partido es **en** el estadio.
*The game is at the stadium.*

✔ **Dentro de** can replace **en** to indicate *into* or *inside*.

El pasaje está **dentro de** la cartera.
*The ticket is inside the purse.*

✔ **En** is used to indicate a definite period of time.

**en** julio, **en** verano, **en** dos meses...
*in July, in summer, within two months...*

Lo terminó **en** diez horas.
*He finished it in ten hours.*

✔ **En** can be used before a noun to indicate means of transport.

Anduve **en** bicicleta.          Viajó **en** auto.
*I rode my bike.*                  *He traveled by car.*

✔ **En** can be used as a synonym for **sobre** *(on)*.

El vaso está **en** (sobre) la mesa.
*The glass is on the table.*

### 7-2a  Verbs requiring the preposition *en*

| | | | |
|---|---|---|---|
| consentir *to agree, consent* | consistir *to consist* | convenir *to agree, admit* | convertirse *to become* |
| demorar *to delay* | empeñarse *to insist* | entrar *to enter* | fijarse *to notice* |
| insistir *to insist* | pensar *to think* | quedar *to agree* | tardar *to delay* |

Quedamos **en** encontrarnos aquí.          El avión tardó **en** llegar.
*We agreed to meet here.*                   *The plane was delayed.*

## 7-3  Use of the preposition *de*

✔ **De** is used to indicate a precise date.

La Declaración de la Independencia de Chile data **de** 1818.
*Chile's Declaration of Independence dates from 1818.*

✔ To indicate possession or belonging, use **noun + de + noun**.

El perro es **de** Juan.          la ventana **de** la casa
*The dog is Juan's.*               *the window of the house*

✔ **De** is used to indicate starting point or place of origin.

Viajaremos **de** Buenos Aires a Río.
*We will travel from Buenos Aires to Río.*

Vengo **de** Valencia. Soy **de** España.
*I come from Valencia. I am from Spain.*

✔ **De** is used to tell of what material things are made.

La silla es **de** madera.
*The chair is made of wood.*

✔ **De** is used to indicate subject or theme.

Nosferatus es una película **de** terror.
*Nosferatus is a horror movie.*

Hablaremos **de** la obra de Julia Álvarez.
*We will talk about Julia Álvarez's work.*

✔ **De** is added to some adverbs of place to change them into prepositions.

*cerca **de**, lejos **de**, delante **de**, detrás **de**, a la izquierda/derecha **de**, encima/debajo **de**, alrededor **de**, dentro/fuera **de**, al lado **de***

✔ **De** is placed between an adjective and an infinitive in impersonal sentences.

Es imposible **de** leer.
*It is impossible to read.*

Es difícil **de** aceptar.
*It is difficult to accept.*

Es fácil **de** explicar.
*It is easy to explain.*

### 7-3a   Verbs requiring the preposition *de*

| | | | |
|---|---|---|---|
| acordarse | alegrarse | arrepentirse | avergonzarse |
| *to remember* | *to be happy* | *to repent* | *to be ashamed* |
| burlarse | dejar | depender | enamorarse |
| *to make fun of* | *to stop* | *to depend* | *to fall in love* |
| enterarse | olvidarse | quejarse | reírse |
| *to find out* | *to forget* | *to complain* | *to laugh about* |

¡Deja **de** hablar!
*Stop talking!*

Pedro depende **de** sus padres.
*Pedro depends on his parents.*

## 7-4 Por/para

### 7-4a Por

Generally the preposition **por** is used to express motion through or by a place, length or duration of time, source, cause, or means. It can be associated with the question **¿por qué?** *(why?).*

✔ Por means *for* in the sense of *for the sake of, on behalf of, in place of.*

Lo hice **por** mis hijos.
*I did it for my children.*

Puedo trabajar **por** ti hoy, pero no mañana.
*I can work for you today, but not tomorrow.*

✔ **Por** means *in exchange for.*

Lo vendí **por** treinta monedas de plata.
*I sold it for thirty silver coins.*

Pagué treinta dólares **por** la bicicleta.
*I paid thirty dollars for the bike.*

✔ **Por** indicates *during, for a period of time, in,* or *for part of the day* when no hour is mentioned.

Tengo que trabajar **por** tres horas.
*I have to work for three hours.*

Estuvo aquí **por** la mañana.
*He/She was here in the morning.*

Nos quedaremos en San Juan **por** dos meses.
*We will stay in San Juan for two months.*

✔ Use **por** to express *in order to get* (with a verb of motion), *in search of, the object of an errand.*

Pasaremos **por** usted mañana a las seis.
*We will pick you up tomorrow at six.*

Fui a la panadería **por** el pan.
*I went to the bakery for the bread.*

✔ **Por** is used to express erroneous identity.

Lo tomaron **por** su hermano.
*They mistook him for his brother.*

✔ **Por** also indicates a general physical movement in and around a given place such as in the following English equivalents: *along, through, out, around, by, down.*

Caminamos **por** la calle.
*We walked down the street.*

El gato saltó **por** la ventana.
*The cat jumped through the window.*

Pasaremos **por** Nueva Jersey para llegar a Nueva York.
*We will pass through New Jersey to get to New York.*

Paseaba **por** el bosque cuando lo vi.
*I was strolling through the woods when I saw him.*

Fuimos a pasear **por** allí.
*We went for a walk around there.*

Pasamos **por** tu casa a las ocho.
*We passed by your house at eight.*

✔ **Por** is used to express *by means of.*

Fue **por** tren de Cuzco a Lima y luego **por** avión a Bogotá.
*He/She went by train from Cuzco to Lima, and then by plane to Bogotá.*

Te llamé **por** teléfono.
*I called you on the phone.*

✔ **Por** is used to mean *per, by* (with units of measurement).

Nos reunimos una vez **por** semana.
*We meet once a week.*

5 **por** ciento
*five percent*

En Chile venden las frutas **por** kilo.
*In Chile they sell fruit by the kilogram.*

El auto iba a 100 millas **por** hora.
*The car was going one hundred miles an hour.*

✔ Por can mean *because of, due to.*

Estoy preocupado **por** el examen médico.
*I am worried because or the medical exam.*

Llegamos atrasados **por** culpa de la circulación.
*We arrived late due to the traffic.*

✔ **Por** is used to express *about to.*

Estoy **por** terminar mi nueva canción.
*I am about to finish my new song.*

La película está **por** comenzar.
*The movie is about to begin.*

Common fixed expressions with **por**

| | | | |
|---|---|---|---|
| algo **por** el estilo<br>*something like that* | estar **por**<br>*to be in favor of* | gracias **por**<br>*thanks for* | **por** ahora<br>*for the time being* |
| **por** allí<br>*there* | **por** aquí<br>*here* | **por** cierto<br>*by the way* | **por** completo<br>*completely* |
| **por** desgracia<br>*unfortunately* | **por** ejemplo<br>*for example* | **por** eso<br>*that's why* | **por** el momento<br>*for the moment* |
| **por** favor<br>*please* | **por** fin<br>*at last* | **por** la mañana<br>*in the morning* | **por** lo visto<br>*apparently* |
| **por** la noche<br>*in the evening* | **por** lo general<br>*in general* | **por** la tarde<br>*in the afternoon* | **por** si acaso<br>*just in case* |
| **por** otra parte<br>*on the other hand* | **por** poco<br>*almost* | **por** lo menos<br>*at least* | **por** última vez<br>*for the last time* |
| **por** suerte<br>*fortunately* | **por** supuesto<br>*of course* | **por** primera vez<br>*for the first time* | |
| **por** último<br>*finally* | | **por** todas partes<br>*everywhere* | |

## 7-4b  Para

The preposition **para** expresses a goal, purpose, recipient of an action, destination, time limits or deadlines, comparison with others—stated or implicit—and readiness. It may be associated with the question *why?* in the sense of *for what purpose?*

**Para** expresses destination for a specific person, thing or organization.

✔ **Para** means for, as in *destined for, to be given to.*

> Compré el auto **para** mi hijo.
> *I bought the car for my son.*

> Mi casa de Isla Negra es **para** los sindicatos de Chile.
> *My house in Isla Negra is for the Chilean labor unions.*

✔ **Para** means *for* in the sense of *in the direction of, toward.*

> Ayer partieron **para** Lima.
> *Yesterday they left for Lima.*

✔ **Para** means *for* in the sense of *in the employ of.*

> El Sr. Rivera trabaja **para** el gobierno.
> *Mr. Rivera works for the government.*

✔ **Para** means *by* or *for* when it is used to express a specified future time or deadline.

> Tengo que terminar el proyecto **para** el mes de junio.
> *I must finish the project by June.*

> Necesito la composición **para** el viernes próximo.
> *I need the composition for next Friday.*

✔ Before an infinitive, whenever the *to* means *in order to,* use **para**.

> Estudio **para** (ser) médico.                **Para** tener buena salud hay que hacer ejercicios.
> *I am studying to be a doctor.*               *To be healthy, you must exercise.*

> **Para** comenzar, les hablaré de los objetivos del taller.
> *To begin with, I will talk to you about the goals of the workshop.*

> **Para** terminar, les pido que sigan cuidadosamente todas las instrucciones.
> *To finish, I'll ask you to follow all the instructions.*

✔ **Para** means *to be used for.*

> Compré tazas **para** café.
> *I bought coffee mugs.*

✔ **Para** is used to show capacity.

Es un estacionamiento **para** 500 autos.
*The parking lot can hold up to 500 cars.*

Queremos una mesa **para** ocho.
*We want a table for eight.*

✔ **Para** is used to express *considering, compared with others, in relation to others,* or to make judgements expressing one's opinion.

**Para** él nada es difícil.
*For him nothing is difficult.*

**Para** ser extranjera habla muy bien el inglés
*She speaks English very well for a foreigner.*

**Para** ellos no es muy bueno, **para** mí es excelente.
*For them it is not so good; for me it is excellent.*

✔ **Para** is used to express benefits or harm.

Hacer ejercicio es bueno **para** la salud.
*To exercise is good for your health.*

Exponerse mucho al sol es malo **para** la piel.
*Overexposure to the sun is bad for your skin.*

✔ When used with **estar + infinitive para** expresses readiness.

Estoy listo **para** salir.
*I am ready to leave.*

Common expressions with **para**

¿**Para** qué?
*Why?, For what reason?, What for?*

No es **para** tanto.
*It isn't as bad as that.*

**para** sí
*to oneself*

estar **para**
*to be about to*

**para** siempre
*forever*

Estoy **para** salir.
*I am about to leave.*

| | ABOUT | AT | FOR | FROM | IN | OF | ON | TO | WITH |
|---|---|---|---|---|---|---|---|---|---|
| *to agree* estar de acuerdo | en algo | | | | | | en + algo en + verbo | con algo en + verbo | con algo alguien |
| *angry* estar enojado | con algo | con algo | | | | | | | con alguien |
| *adapted* adaptado | | | para | del | | | | a | |
| *capable* capaz | | | | | | de | | | |
| *to compare* comparar | | | | | | | | a | con |
| *concerned* preocupado | por | | por | | en | | | | con |
| *to consist* consistir/constar | | | | | en | de | | | |
| *convenient* conveniente | | | para | | | | | para | |
| *to decide* decidirse | | | | | | | por/sobre | a hacer algo | |
| *to differ* diferir | acerca de | | | de | en algo | | sobre | | con alguien |
| *different* diferente | | | | de | | | | | |
| *disappointed* decepcionado | | | | | en | | | | con |
| *empty* vacío | | | | | | de | | | |
| *envious* envidioso | | | | | | de | | | |
| *to enter* entrar | | a | para | | en | | | | |
| *to fail* fracasar | | | | | en un intento | | | en hacer algo | con |
| *to live* vivir | | en [casa] | para | | en [ciudad/ país] | | en [calle] de | | |
| *to practice* practicar | | | para | | | | | para | |
| *to regret* lamentar/ se arrepentirse | | | por | de | | | | | |
| *to result* resultar | | | | | en | | | | |
| *sensitive* sensible | | | | | | | | | |
| *to speak* hablar | sobre | | por | | | | de | a | con alguien |
| *sympathy* solidaridad/ compasión | | | por | | | | | a | con |
| *to think* pensar | en | | | | | de | | | |

# CHAPTER 8

## *Indefinites*

**INDEFINITES** are pronouns, adjectives, or adverbials that lack precise limits.

### 8-1 Pronouns

| Positive indefinite pronouns | Negative indefinite pronouns |
|---|---|
| alguien<br>*someone* | nadie<br>*nobody, anyone* |
| alguno(a)/algunos(as)<br>*someone, one/some* | ninguno(a)<br>*no one, nobody* |
| unos(as)<br>*some* | |
| algo<br>*something* | nada<br>*nothing* |
| cualquiera<br>*anybody* | nadie<br>*nobody* |

### 8-2 Adjectives

| Positive indefinite adjectives | Negative indefinite adjectives |
|---|---|
| algún/alguno<br>algunas/algunos<br>*some* | ningún/ninguno<br>*not any* |
| todo(a)<br>*all of* | ninguno(a)/ningunos(as)<br>*not any, no* |

## 8-3 Adverbials

| Positive indefinite adverbials | Negative indefinite adverbials |
|---|---|
| también<br>*also* | tampoco<br>*neither* |
| en alguna parte<br>*somewhere* | en ninguna parte<br>*nowhere* |
| de algún modo<br>*somehow* | de ningún modo<br>*no way* |
| alguna vez<br>*ever, at some time* | nunca<br>*never* |
| algunas veces<br>*sometimes* | raras veces<br>*rarely* |
| una vez<br>*once* | nunca<br>*never* |
| algún día<br>*some day* | jamás<br>*never* |
| siempre<br>*always* | casi nunca<br>*almost never* |
| cada vez<br>*every time* | en ningún momento<br>*at no time* |

# CHAPTER 9

## *Conjunctions*

**Conjunctions** are invariable connecting words used to join words, sentences, or clauses, thereby establishing relationships between them.

**9-1 Coordinating conjunctions** *connect two words, parts of a sentence, groups of words, or prepositions.*

| y/e | pero | o/u | ni | que |
|-----|------|-----|-----|-----|
| *and* | *but* | *or* | *nor* | *that, which, who* |

✔ The conjunction **y** changes to **e** before a word beginning with **i** or **hi**.

**y  →  e**

| | |
|---|---|
| Isabel **y** Luis fueron de pesca. | *Isabel and Luis went fishing.* |
| Luis **e** Isabel fueron al río. | *Luis and Isabel went to the river.* |
| Estudio historia **y** filosofía. | *I study history and philosophy.* |
| Estudio filosofía **e** historia. | *I study philosophy and history.* |

✔ The conjunction **y** doesn't change when the **i** is a semi-consonant.

La nave era de madera **y** hierro.
*The ship was made of wood and iron.*

✔ The conjunction **o** changes to **u** before a word beginning with **o** or **ho**.

**o  →  u**

Necesitamos siete **u** ocho botellas de agua.
*We need seven or eight bottles of water.*

—¿Amor **u** honor?— se preguntó el caballero de la triste figura.
—Amor— le respondió Dulcinea mientras siete **u** ocho molinos aplaudían.
*"Love or honor?" Don Quijote asked himself. "Love" answered Dulcinea while seven or eight windmills applauded.*

✔ The conjunction **ni** is only used in negative sentences.

No baila **ni** canta.
*He doesn't dance or sing. He neither dances nor sings.*

### 9-2 **Conjunctions of time** *express previousness, simultaneity or posteriority.*

| | | | |
|---|---|---|---|
| cuando | antes de que | después de que | hasta que |
| *when* | *before* | *after* | *until* |
| tan pronto como | en cuanto | mientras que | |
| *as soon as* | *as soon as* | *while* | |

✔ To describe an action that is pending and that may or may not take place, use a conjunction of time followed by the subjunctive.

**Cuando** suba al avión dormiré.
*When I get on the plane, I will sleep.*

✔ To describe a habitual or a completed action, use the conjunction of time with the indicative.

**Cuando** subo al avión duermo.         **Cuando** subí al avión dormí.
*When I get on the plane I sleep.*        *When I got on the plane I slept.*

✔ The conjunction **antes de que** is always followed by a verb in the subjunctive even when it describes habitual actions.

Todos los días limpio la mesa **antes de que coman** los niños.
*Every day I clean the table before the children eat.*

### 9-3 **Conjunctions of purpose** *link an independent clause to a dependent clause.*

| | | |
|---|---|---|
| a menos que | con tal que | en caso que |
| *unless* | *provided that* | *in case* |
| para que | que | sin que |
| *so, so that, in order to* | *that* | *without* |

Iremos al cine **con tal que** tengamos tiempo.
*We will go to the movies provided we have time.*

**9-4 Subordinating** *or* **adverbial conjunctions** *link a subordinate clause to the main clause.*

| | | | |
|---|---|---|---|
| después que<br>*after* | aunque<br>*although* | como<br>*as* | como si<br>*as if* |
| tanto como/mientras<br>*as long as* | en cuanto<br>*as soon as* | porque<br>*because* | antes de<br>*before* |
| si<br>*if* | para que<br>*in order that* | ahora<br>*now* | desde<br>*since* |
| así que<br>*so that* | que<br>*that* | mientras<br>*while* | a menos que<br>*unless* |
| hasta que<br>*until* | cuando<br>*when* | donde<br>*where* | en cuanto<br>*as soon as* |

✔ Subordinating conjunctions can be used with the indicative to describe habitual actions or known facts.

Mi marido siempre lee **cuando** llega.
*My husband always reads when he comes home.*

✔ Subordinating conjunctions are used with the subjunctive when the expressions describe a future or hypothetical action.

Mi marido comerá **en cuanto** llegue a casa.
*My husband will eat as soon as he gets home.*

**9-5 Adversative conjunctions** *express antithesis or opposition.*

| pero<br>*but* | sino<br>*on the contrary, rather* | sino que<br>*but, instead* | sin embargo<br>*nevertheless* |
|---|---|---|---|

**Pero** is a conjunction that links affirmative or negative sentences.

✔ If the statement preceding **pero** is affirmative, **pero** means *but*.

Él tiene mucho dinero **pero** viste mal.
*He has a lot of money, but dresses poorly.*

—Soy pobre **pero** honrado—, dijo Chavalillo muriendo de hambre.
*"I am poor but honest," said Chavalillo, starving.*

✔ If the statement preceding **pero** is negative, **pero** means *but* in the sense of *nevertheless* or *however*.

Ella no tiene mucho dinero **pero** viste bien.
*She doesn't have a lot of money, but dresses well.*

✔ **Sino** and **sino que** are used when contrasting two statements; the first one in the negative form and the second one in the affirmative form.

✔ **Sino** is equivalent to *on the contrary, rather,* or *instead,* and is used to introduce a contrary idea after a negative statement.

No fuimos a las montañas **sino** al mar.
*We did not go to the mountains but rather to the sea.*

No es por Rosario Ferré **sino** por Ana Lydia Vega.
*It is not by Rosario Ferré but by Ana Lydia Vega.*

✔ When a verb follows **sino,** it must be in the infinitive.

No le gusta tocar el piano **sino** jugar al básquetbol.
*He doesn't like to play the piano, but to play basketball.*

✔ If a conjugated verb is used with **sino, que** must be used between **sino** and the verb.

Ellos no escuchan música clásica **sino que** escuchan música folk.
*They don't listen to classical music, but to folk music.*

Del miedo que le dio, no caminó **sino que** corrió.
*He was so scared that he didn't walk, but ran.*

✔ Sin embargo *(nevertheless)* is used to contrast two statements.

Se levantó muy temprano, **sin embargo** llegó con retraso.
*He got up very early; nevertheless he was late.*

# CHAPTER 10

## *Interrogative Words*

**Interrogative words** are words used to ask a question. They require a written accent mark and two question marks. ¿ . . . ?

| | | | |
|---|---|---|---|
| ¿Qué...? <br> *What . . . ?* | ¿De qué...? <br> *What . . . about/from?* | ¿Cuál...? <br> *Which (one) . . . ?* | ¿Cuáles...? <br> *Which (ones) . . . ?* |
| ¿Cómo...? <br> *How . . . ?* | ¿Cuándo...? <br> *When . . . ?* | ¿Dónde...? <br> *Where . . . ?* | ¿De dónde? <br> *Where . . . from?* |
| ¿A dónde...? <br> *Where . . . to?* | ¿Por qué...? <br> *Why . . . ?* | ¿Cuánto...? <br> *How much . . . ?* | ¿Cuánto/os/as...? <br> *How many . . . ?* |
| ¿Quién...? <br> *Who . . . ?* | ¿Quiénes...? <br> *Who . . . (plural)* | ¿De quién...? <br> *Whose . . . ?* | ¿De quiénes? <br> *Whose . . . ?* |

### 10-1  ¿qué?/¿cuál?

✔ In general, **qué** is equivalent to *what* and **cuál** is equivalent to *which*, except when followed by the verb **ser**.

✔ ¿**Qué**? expresses *what?* when it asks for a definition or an explanation.

¿**Qué** + verb?

| | |
|---|---|
| ¿**Qué** quieres? | *What do you want?* |
| ¿**Qué** haces? | *What are you doing?* |
| ¿**Qué** es esto? | *What is this?* |

¿**Preposition + qué + verb?**

¿En **qué** piensas? <br>
*What are you thinking about?*

✔ **¿Qué?** + **ser** expresses *what?* and asks for a definition, an identification, a classification, or an explanation.

**¿Qué eres,** hondureño o colombiano?
*What are you, Honduran or Colombian?*

**¿Qué es** la vida? Un frenesí. **¿Qué es** la vida? Una ilusión.
*What is life? It is a frenzy. What is life? It is an illusion.*

(Calderón de la Barca, *La vida es sueño*)

✔ **¿Qué?** can be directly followed by a noun.

**¿Qué corbata** quieres ponerte?        **¿Qué clase** prefieres?
*What tie do you want to wear?*           *What class do you prefer?*

## 10-2 ¿Cuál(es)? + ser *asks what? in the sense of* which one?

**¿Cuál** es tu clase favorita?           **¿Cuál** es la capital de Chile?
*What is your favorite class?*            *What is the capital of Chile?*

✔ **¿Cuál(es)?** used alone expresses *which one?* and implies selection from a group.

**¿Cuál?** (**¿Cuál prefieres,** la roja o la blanca?)
*Which one? (Which one do you prefer; the red or the white?)*

**¿Cuál + de + noun?**

**¿Cuál** de los poemas te gustó más?
*Which one of the poems did you like the best?*

# CHAPTER 11

## *Exclamatory Words*

**Exclamatory words** are the same as the interrogative words: **quién, cuánto, cómo** and **qué**, but used to express strong emotions such as surprise, joy, or indignation.

✔ Exclamatory words require a written accent mark and enclosing exclamation points.  ¡ . . . !

    **¡Quién...!**    **¡Cómo...!**    **¡Cuánto...!**    **¡Qué...!**    **¡Cuán...!**

✔ **¡Quién + imperfect/past-pluperfect subjunctive!** expresses a personal wish in an impersonal way.

    **¡Quién** <u>pudiera</u> volar!                **¡Quién** lo <u>hubiera adivinado</u>!
    *I wish I could fly!*                  *Who would have guessed!*

### 11-1 Exclamatory sentences with adjective or adverb

✔ **¡Qué/cuán + adjective** or **adverb!** means *how.*

    **¡Qué** <u>bonito</u>! *How pretty!*

    **¡Qué** <u>mal</u> me siento! *How badly I feel!*

    **¡Cuán** <u>feliz</u> soy! *How happy I am!*

    **¡Cuán** <u>rápido</u> va este auto! *How fast this car goes!*

### 11-2 Exclamatory sentences with nouns

✔ **¡Qué/cuánto + noun!** means *what.*

    **¡Qué** <u>alegría</u>! *What joy!*

    **¡Cuánta** <u>gente</u> hay aquí! *What a crowd!*

Notice the syntax when **qué** is used with a modified noun.

**¡Qué + noun + más/tan + adjective!**

**¡Qué** (novela) **tan** (extraordinaria!)
*What an extraordinary novel!*

*or*

**¡Qué + noun + más/tan + adj + verb!**

**¡Qué** niña **tan** inteligente es ésta!
*What an intelligent girl she is!*

## 11-3 Exclamatory sentences with verbs

✔ **¡Cómo/cuánto + verb!** means *how (in what manner)*.

| | |
|---|---|
| **¡Cómo** se divierten los niños! | **¡Cuánto** te amo! |
| *How much fun the kids are having!* | *How (much) I love you!* |

# CHAPTER 12

## *Accentuation*

✔ In Spanish all the words have a syllable that is stressed.

### 12-1 Rules for stressing words

Where are words stressed?

✔ If the word ends in a **vowel,** or the **consonants -n** or **-s,** it is stressed on the next-to-the-last syllable. (Each ☐ square represents a syllable.)

If the shaded box represents the stressed syllable, **amigo** would look like this:

☐ ■ ☐

The boldface letters in the words below show that the stress falls in the next-to-last syllable (because each of these words ends with a vowel or the **consonants -n** or **-s**).

**ca**sa      ca**mi**nen      **a**ños

✔ If a word ends in a consonant other than **-n** or **-s,** it is stressed on the last syllable.

The verb **esperar** would look like this:

☐ ☐ ■

Like **esperar,** the following words end in a **consonant** other than **-n** or **-s**

espa**ñol**      lu**gar**      na**riz**

### 12-2 Written accent

When do words require a written accent?

✔ Words that do not follow the aforementioned rules require a written accent to indicate where the stress is placed.

✔ Words stressed on the last syllable are called **agudas.** When they end in a **vowel, -n,** or **-s,** they require an accent.

**Autobús** is a word of this type. If each square is used to represent a syllable, it would look like this:

☐ ☐ ■

papá     patrón     japonés

✔ Words stressed on the next-to-the-last syllable are called **graves** or **llanas.** If they end in a **consonant** other than **-n** or **-s,** they require an accent.

**Difícil** is an example of this type of word. Using boxes to represent syllables, it would look like this:

☐ ■ ☐

árbol     césped     fútbol

✔ Words stressed two (**esdrújulas**) or three syllables (**sobreesdrújulas**) before the last syllable always take a written accent.

**Último** is an **esdrújula** word. This is how it would look with boxes representing each syllable:

■ ☐ ☐

música     dímelo     árboles

**Dígamelo** is a **sobreesdrújula** word. This is how it would look with boxes representing each syllable:

■ ☐ ☐ ☐

✔ When a singular word becomes plural, the placement of the stress usually does not change.

ágil          ágiles

amarillo     amarillos

There are exceptions. For example:

carácter     caracteres

régimen     regímenes

✔ Changes in word endings will determine if and where a written accent is required even though the stressed syllable stays the same. In the plural or the feminine the written accent may no longer be necessary.

inglés
*Englishman*

inglesa
*Englishwoman*

acción
*action*

acciones
*actions*

alemán
*German man*

alemana
*German woman*

✔ In some verbal forms, when a syllable is added, a written accent is required to indicate the stress has not moved.

leyendo       leyéndolo

✔ The written accent also allows one to distinguish between words written identically but with different meaning.

| el | *(the)* | article | él | *(he)* | personal pronoun |
|----|---------|---------|-----|--------|------------------|
| si | *(if)* | conjunction | sí | *(yes)* | adverb |
| mas | *(in addition to)* | conjunction | más | *(more)* | adverb |
| solo | *(alone, unique)* | adjective | sólo | *(only)* | adverb |
| de | *(of, from)* | preposition | dé | *(I gave)* | verb **dar** |
| se | *(one, passive voice)* | pronoun | sé | *(I know)* | verb **saber** |

✔ Accents distinguish demonstrative pronouns from demonstrative adjectives.

*Note:* According to the new rules of the Real Academia Española, the written accent on the demonstrative pronouns is optional.

| demonstrative adjectives | demonstrative pronouns |
|--------------------------|------------------------|
| este(a) | éste(a) |
| ese(a) | ése(a) |
| aquel(la) | aquél(la) |

✔ All the interrogative and exclamatory words have a written accent mark.

| ¿dónde? | ¿adónde? | ¿cuándo? |
|---------|----------|----------|
| ¿cómo? | ¿cuánto? | ¿cuál/es? |
| ¿qué? | ¿por qué? | ¿quién/es? |

✔ *Note*: In current language use, the written accent on capital letters is optional.

# CHAPTER 13

## Diphthongs and Triphthongs

**13-1 Diphthongs** *are single syllables formed by the combination of two vowels.*

✔ Three combinations are possible.

| strong-weak | weak-strong | weak-weak |
|---|---|---|
| a/e/o combined with i/u | i/u combined with -a/e/o | i/u |

| | | |
|---|---|---|
| ai/ei/oi | ia/ie/io | iu |
| au/eu/ou | ua/ue/uo | ui |

✔ A written accent is required to separate diphthongs into two syllables.

✔ The written accent is placed on the stressed syllable.

✔ In the combination of strong and weak, if the weak vowel is stressed, it must have a written accent.

| feria | baile | reina | aula | seudo | oiga | cuidado |
|---|---|---|---|---|---|---|
| alegría | maíz | reír | reúna | baúl | oído | huí |

**13-2 Triphthongs** *are single syllables formed by the combination of three vowels.*

### weak — strong — weak

| wsw | wsw | wsw | wsw |
|---|---|---|---|
| uey | uay | iei | iai |
| | Uruguay | estudiéis | estudiáis |
| buey | Paraguay | enjuiciéis | enjuiciáis |

✔ If the first weak vowel is stressed, it must have a written accent.

esperaríais        miraríais

# CHAPTER 14

## *Syllabication*

✔ All Spanish words are divided into as many syllables as they have vowel sounds (vowel, diphthong, or triphthong)

### 14-1  How to divide into syllables

✔ If there is a vowel or diphthong at the beginning of a word, followed by a consonant, divide after the vowel or diphthong.

**vowel or diphthong ÷ consonant**

a ño          au ricular          e mérito

✔ If there is a vowel at the beginning of a word followed by two consonants, divide between the consonants.

**vowel + consonant ÷ consonant**

ac ción          ac tivar          ag nóstico

*but* if the word has a **vowel + consonant + l** or **r,** divide after the vowel.

a climatarse          A crópolis

✔ If there is a consonant and a vowel divide after the vowel.

**consonant + vowel ÷**

*pa pá*          *li bro*          *me se ro*

*Note:* ch, **ll** and **rr** are considered single consonants.

Chi le          po llo          pe rro

✔ If there are two consonants, divide between the consonants.

**consonant ÷ consonant**

can tar          car gar

*but*

**consonant + l or r ÷**

cannot be divided, with the exception of **sl** and **sr.**

ha **bl**ar          ha **br**á

ais **l**an te          **Is** rael

✔ If there are three consonants, divide before the last consonant.

**Consonant + consonant ÷ consonant**

ins **t**i tu ción

*but*

If the second consonant is followed by **l** or **r,** divide after the first consonant.

**consonant ÷ consonant + l or r**

com **pl**e men to          com **pr**en der

✔ If there are four consonants, divide in the middle.

**consonant + consonant ÷ consonant + consonant**

cons **tr**uc tor          ins **tr**uc tor

**Basic patterns you need to remember.**

✔ ¿Cómo se llama usted? *(you, formal)* or ¿Cómo te llamas? *(you, informal)*
*What is your name?*

Me llamo John/Mary.
*My name is John/Mary.*

✗ **never:** Me llamo **es** John/Mary.

✔ ¿Cuál es su/tu nacionalidad?          Soy americano(a).
*What is your nationality?*          *I am American.*

**but:** español(**a**), francés/frances**a**, canadiense/canadiense
*Spanish, French, Canadian respectively*

✔ ¿De dónde es/eres?          Soy de los Estados Unidos.
*Where are you from?*          *I am from the United States.*

✔ ¿Cuántos años tiene/tienes?
*How old are you?*

Tengo 19 años.
*I am nineteen years old.*

✔ ¿Qué estudia/estudias?
*What do you study?*

Estudio español y negocios.
*I study Spanish and business.*

✔ ¿Dónde vive/vives?
*Where do you live?*

Vivo en la calle 33 en la ciudad de Nueva York.
*I live at 33rd Street, New York City.*

✔ ¿Cómo es/eres?
*What are you like? (Describe yourself)*

Soy alto/a, (bajo/a), delgado/a, (gordo/a), simpático/a, inteligente y muy optimista.
*I am tall/short, thin/fat, nice, intelligent and very optimistic.*

*but* Tengo el pelo largo/corto, lacio/rizado, negro/rubio y los ojos verdes/azules/ color café.
*I have long/short, straight/curly, black/blond hair, and green/blue/brown eyes.*

✔ ¿Cómo está usted? or ¿Cómo estás?
*How are you?*

Estoy bien, gracias.
*I am fine, thank you.*

Estoy un poco enfermo(a).
*I am a little sick.*

✔ ¿Quién es ella?
*Who is she?*

Es la profesora de español.
*She is the Spanish professor.*

✔ ¿Quién es él?
*Who is he?*

Es un estudiante.
*He is a student.*

✔ ¿Quién es ella?
*Who is she?*

Es una estudiante.
*She is a student.*

✔ ¿Quiénes son ellos?
*Who are they?*

Son Paty y Juan, son estudiantes.
*They are Paty and Juan; they are students.*

✔ ¿Cuándo nació/naciste?
*When were you born?*

Nací el 5 de enero de 19-
*I was born on the 5th of January, 19-*

✔ ¿Dónde nació/naciste?
*Where were you born?*

Nací en Dallas, Texas.
*I was born in Dallas, Texas.*

✔ ¿Qué le/te gusta hacer?
*What do you like to do?*

¿Me gusta viajar, leer, e ir a bailar los sábados por la noche.
*I like to travel, read, and go dancing on Saturday night.*

*but:* me gusta **hacer** ejercicio.

✔ ¿Qué idiomas habla/hablas?
*What languages do you speak?*

Hablo inglés y un poco de español.
*I speak English and a little bit of Spanish.*

*but* Hablo **el** inglés correctamente.
*I speak English correctly.*

✔ ¿Qué hora es?
*What time is it?*

**Es** la una. **Son** las cinco.
*It is one o'clock. It is five o'clock.*

✔ ¿Qué está/estás haciendo? (hacer)
*What are you doing? (to do/make)*

Luis está comiendo. (comer)
*Luis is eating. (to eat)*

Estoy estudiando. (estudiar)
*I am studying. (to study)*

✔ ¿Qué hace/haces en la mañana?
*What do you do in the morning?*

En la mañana me despierto, me levanto, me ducho, me peino, me visto, estudio, y me voy para mi clase de español.
*In the morning I wake up, get up, take a shower, comb my hair, get dressed, study, and leave for my Spanish class.*

✔ Qué va/vas a hacer?
*What are you going to do?*

(Yo) Voy a estudiar el verbo **ir.** Luis (él) va a repasar el futuro. Luego (nosotros) vamos a ir al cine a ver *La casa de los espíritus.*
*I am going to study the verb ir. Luis is going to review the future tense. Then, we are going to the movies to see* The House of the Spirits.

**ir:** voy/vas/va  vamos/vais/van

# INDEX OF VERBS

*Regular, Stem-Changing, Irregular, and Reflexive Verbs*

*Note:* Numbers indicate where each verb is located in the verb index.

# INDEX OF VERBS

*Regular, Stem-Changing, Irregular, and Reflexive Verbs*

## REGULAR VERBS

**1. Regular -ar verbs:** *amar*, acabar, ahorrar, aconsejar, bailar, cambiar, caminar, cantar, cocinar, comentar, comprar, contestar, conversar, cortar, dejar, desear, enseñar, esperar, estudiar, hablar, interesar, invitar, lavar(se), levantar(se), llevar, llorar, mirar, nadar, necesitar, olvidar, practicar, preguntar, trabajar, tardar, usar

| PRESENT | PRETERITE | IMPERFECT | FUTURE | CONDITIONAL | PRESENT SUBJUNCTIVE | IMPERFECT SUBJUNCTIVE | IMPERATIVE |
|---|---|---|---|---|---|---|---|
| am o | am é | am aba | amar é | amar ía | am e | ama ra | |
| am as | am aste | am abas | amar ás | amar ías | am es | ama ras | ama/no ames |
| am a | am ó | am aba | amar á | amar ía | am e | ama ra | ame (Ud.) |
| am amos | am amos | am ábamos | amar emos | amar íamos | am emos | amá ramos | amemos |
| am áis | am asteis | am abais | amar éis | amar íais | am éis | ama rais | amad/no améis |
| am an | am aron | am aban | amar án | amar ían | am en | ama ran | amen |

Infinitive: am **ar**     Present participle (gerund): am **ando**     Past participle: am **ado**

**2. Regular -er verbs:** *comer*, aprender, beber, comprender, correr, deber, depender, emprender, meter, prender, responder, romper, vender

| PRESENT | PRETERITE | IMPERFECT | FUTURE | CONDITIONAL | PRESENT SUBJUNCTIVE | IMPERFECT SUBJUNCTIVE | IMPERATIVE |
|---|---|---|---|---|---|---|---|
| com o | com í | com ía | comer é | comer ía | com a | comie ra | |
| com es | com iste | com ías | comer ás | comer ías | com as | comie ras | come/no comas |
| com e | com ió | com ía | comer á | comer ía | com a | comie ra | coma (Ud.) |
| com emos | com imos | com íamos | comer emos | comer íamos | com amos | comié ramos | comamos |
| com éis | com isteis | com íais | comer éis | comer íais | com áis | comie rais | comed |
| com en | com ieron | com ían | comer án | comer ían | com an | comie ran | coman |

Infinitive: com **er**     Present participle (gerund): com **iendo**     Past participle: com **ido**

**3. Regular -ir verbs:** *vivir*, abrir, acudir, añadir, aplaudir, asistir (a), compartir, decidir, describir, discutir, emitir, escribir, insistir (en), permitir, recibir, resumir

| PRESENT | PRETERITE | IMPERFECT | FUTURE | CONDITIONAL | PRESENT SUBJUNCTIVE | IMPERFECT SUBJUNCTIVE | IMPERATIVE |
|---|---|---|---|---|---|---|---|
| viv o | viv í | viv ía | vivir é | vivir ía | viv a | vivie ra | |
| viv es | viv iste | viv ías | vivir ás | vivir ías | viv as | vivie ras | vive/no vivas |
| viv e | viv ió | viv ía | vivir á | vivir ía | viv a | vivie ra | viva (Ud.) |
| viv imos | viv imos | viv íamos | vivir emos | vivir íamos | viv amos | vivié ramos | vivamos |
| viv ís | viv isteis | viv íais | vivir éis | vivir íais | viv áis | vivie rais | vivid/no viváis |
| viv en | viv ieron | viv ían | vivir án | vivir ían | viv an | vivie ran | vivan |

Infinitive: viv **ir**     Present participle (gerund): viv **iendo**     Past participle: viv **ido**

# 4. Compound tenses: the correspondent tense of **haber + past participle**

| PRESENT PERFECT | | PAST PERFECT | | PLUPERFECT | | FUTURE PERFECT | | CONDITIONAL PERFECT | | PRESENT PERFECT SUBJUNCTIVE | | PLUPERFECT SUBJUNCTIVE | |
|---|---|---|---|---|---|---|---|---|---|---|---|---|---|
| he | am ado | hube | am ado | había | am ado | habré | am ado | habría | am ado | haya | am ado | hubiera | am ado |
| has | com ido | hubiste | com ido | habías | com ido | habrás | com ido | habrías | com ido | hayas | com ido | hubieras | com ido |
| ha | | hubo | | había | | habrá | | habría | | haya | | hubiera | |
| hemos | | hubimos | | habíamos | | habremos | | habríamos | | hayamos | | hubiéramos | |
| habéis | | hubisteis | | habíais | | habréis | | habríais | | hayáis | | hubierais | |
| han | viv ido | hubieron | viv ido | habían | viv ido | habrán | viv ido | habrían | viv ido | hayan | viv ido | hubieran | viv ido |

# STEM-CHANGING VERBS

## 5. -ar stem-changing verbs in the present (e → ie) *cerrar*, acertar, calentar, despertar(se), encerrar, gobernar, quebrar(se), recomendar, pensar, sentar(se)

| PRESENT | PRETERITE | IMPERFECT | FUTURE | CONDITIONAL | PRESENT SUBJUNCTIVE | IMPERFECT SUBJUNCTIVE | IMPERATIVE |
|---|---|---|---|---|---|---|---|
| cierr o | cerr é | cerr aba | cerrar é | cerrar ía | cierr e | cerra ra | |
| cierr as | cerr aste | cerr abas | cerrar ás | cerrar ías | cierr es | cerra ras | cierra/no cierres |
| cierr a | cerr ó | cerr aba | cerrar á | cerrar ía | cierr e | cerra ra | cierre (Ud.) |
| cerr amos | cerr amos | cerr ábamos | cerrar emos | cerrar íamos | cerr emos | cerrá ramos | cerremos |
| cerr áis | cerr asteis | cerr abais | cerrar éis | cerrar íais | cerr éis | cerra rais | cerrad/no cerréis |
| cierr an | cerr aron | cerr aban | cerrar án | cerrar ían | cierr en | cerrar an | |

**Compound tenses:** they are formed with the correspondent tenses of **haber + past participle**

| PRESENT PERFECT | PAST PERFECT | PLUPERFECT | FUTURE PERFECT | CONDITIONAL PERFECT | PRESENT PERFECT SUBJUNCTIVE | PLUPERFECT SUBJUNCTIVE |
|---|---|---|---|---|---|---|
| **he** cerrado | **hube** cerrado | **había** cerrado | **habré** cerrado | **habría** cerrado | **haya** cerrado | **hubiera** cerrado |

## 6. -er stem-changing verbs in the present (e → ie) *perder*, atender, defender, encender, entender, tender

| PRESENT | PRETERITE | IMPERFECT | FUTURE | CONDITIONAL | PRESENT SUBJUNCTIVE | IMPERFECT SUBJUNCTIVE | IMPERATIVE |
|---|---|---|---|---|---|---|---|
| pierd o | perd í | perd ía | perder é | perder ía | pierd a | perdie ra | |
| pierd es | perd iste | perd ías | perder ás | perder ías | pierd as | perdie ras | pierde/no pierdas |
| pierd e | perd ió | perd ía | perder á | perder ía | pierd a | perdie ra | pierda (Ud.) |
| perd emos | perd imos | perd íamos | perder emos | perder íamos | perd amos | perdié ramos | perdamos |
| perd éis | perd isteis | perd íais | perder éis | perder íais | perd áis | perdie rais | perded/no perdáis |
| pierd en | perd ieron | perd ían | perder án | perder ían | pierd an | perdie ran | pierdan |

| PRESENT PERFECT | PAST PERFECT | PLUPERFECT | FUTURE PERFECT | CONDITIONAL PERFECT | PRESENT PERFECT SUBJUNCTIVE | PLUPERFECT SUBJUNCTIVE |
|---|---|---|---|---|---|---|
| **he** perdido | **hube** perdido | **había** perdido | **habré** perdido | **habría** perdido | **haya** perdido | **hubiera** perdido |

## 7. -*ir* stem-changing verbs in the present (e → ie) *sentir*, arrepentirse, divertir(se), herir(se), mentir, preferir, sugerir

| PRESENT | PRETERITE | IMPERFECT | FUTURE | CONDITIONAL | PRESENT SUBJUNCTIVE | IMPERFECT SUBJUNCTIVE | IMPERATIVE |
|---|---|---|---|---|---|---|---|
| sient o | sent í | sent ía | sentir é | sentir ía | sient a | sintie ra | |
| sient es | sent iste | sent ías | sentir ás | sentir ías | sient as | sintie ras | siente/no sientas |
| sient e | sint ió | sent ía | sentir á | sentir ía | sient a | sintie ra | sienta (Ud.) |
| sent imos | sent imos | sent íamos | sentir emos | sentir íamos | sint amos | sintié ramos | sintamos |
| sent ís | sent isteis | sent íais | sentir éis | sentir íais | sint áis | sintie rais | sentid/no sintáis |
| sient en | sint ieron | sent ían | sentir án | sentir ían | sient an | sintie ran | sientan |

| PRESENT PERFECT | PAST PERFECT | PLUPERFECT | FUTURE PERFECT | CONDITIONAL PERFECT | PRESENT PERFECT SUBJUNCTIVE | PLUPERFECT SUBJUNCTIVE |
|---|---|---|---|---|---|---|
| he sentido | hube sentido | había sentido | habré sentido | habría sentido | haya sentido | hubiera sentido |

## 8. -*ir* stem-changing verbs in the present (e → i) *pedir*, competir, desvestir(se), despedir(se), medir, repetir, servir, vestir(se)

| PRESENT | PRETERITE | IMPERFECT | FUTURE | CONDITIONAL | PRESENT SUBJUNCTIVE | IMPERFECT SUBJUNCTIVE | IMPERATIVE |
|---|---|---|---|---|---|---|---|
| pid o | ped í | ped ía | pedir é | pedir ía | pid a | pidie ra | |
| pid es | ped iste | ped ías | pedir ás | pedir ías | pid as | pidie ras | pide/ no pidas |
| pid e | pid ió | ped ía | pedir á | pedir ía | pid a | pidie ra | pida (Ud.) |
| ped imos | ped imos | ped íamos | pedir emos | pedir íamos | pid amos | pidié ramos | pidamos |
| ped ís | ped isteis | ped íais | pedir éis | pedir íais | pid áis | pidie rais | pedid/no pidáis |
| pid en | pid ieron | ped ían | pedir án | pedir ían | pid an | pidie ran | pidan |

| PRESENT PERFECT | PAST PERFECT | PLUPERFECT | FUTURE PERFECT | CONDITIONAL PERFECT | PRESENT PERFECT SUBJUNCTIVE | PLUPERFECT SUBJUNCTIVE |
|---|---|---|---|---|---|---|
| he pedido | hube pedido | había pedido | habré pedido | habría pedido | haya pedido | hubiera pedido |

## 9. -*ar* stem-changing verbs in the present (o → ue) *contar*, acordar(se), acostar(se), costar, encontrar, mostrar, probar, recordar, sonar, soñar

| PRESENT | PRETERITE | IMPERFECT | FUTURE | CONDITIONAL | PRESENT SUBJUNCTIVE | IMPERFECT SUBJUNCTIVE | IMPERATIVE |
|---|---|---|---|---|---|---|---|
| cuent o | cont é | cont aba | contar é | contar ía | cuent e | conta ra | |
| cuent as | cont aste | cont abas | contar ás | contar ías | cuent es | conta ras | cuenta/no cuentes |
| cuent a | cont ó | cont aba | contar á | contar ía | cuent e | conta ra | cuente (Ud.) |
| cont amos | cont amos | cont ábamos | contar emos | contar íamos | cont emos | contá ramos | contemos |
| cont áis | cont asteis | cont abais | contar éis | contar íais | cont éis | conta rais | contad/no contéis |
| cuent an | cont aron | cont aban | contar án | contar ían | cuent en | contar an | cuenten |

| PRESENT PERFECT | PAST PERFECT | PLUPERFECT | FUTURE PERFECT | CONDITIONAL PERFECT | PRESENT PERFECT SUBJUNCTIVE | PLUPERFECT SUBJUNCTIVE |
|---|---|---|---|---|---|---|
| he contado | hube contado | había contado | habré contado | habría contado | haya contado | hubiera contado |

## 10. -*ar* stem-changing verbs (u → ü) in front of e *averiguar*, amortiguar, apaciguar, atestiguar

| PRESENT | PRETERITE | IMPERFECT | FUTURE | CONDITIONAL | PRESENT SUBJUNCTIVE | IMPERFECT SUBJUNCTIVE | IMPERATIVE |
|---|---|---|---|---|---|---|---|
| averigu o | averigü é | averigu aba | averiguar é | averiguar ía | averigü e | averigua ra | |
| averigu as | averigu aste | averigu abas | averiguar ás | averiguar ías | averigü es | averigua ras | averigua/no averigües |
| averigu a | averigu ó | averigu aba | averiguar á | averiguar ía | averigü e | averigua ra | averigüe (Ud.) |
| averigu amos | averigu amos | averigu ábamos | averiguar emos | averiguar íamos | averigü emos | averiguá ramos | averigüemos |
| averigu áis | averigu asteis | averigu abais | averiguar éis | averiguar íais | averigü éis | averigua rais | averiguad/no averigüéis |
| averigu an | averigu aron | averigu aban | averiguar án | averiguar ían | averigü en | averigua ran | averigüen |

| PRESENT PERFECT | PAST PERFECT | PLUPERFECT | FUTURE PERFECT | CONDITIONAL PERFECT | PRESENT PERFECT SUBJUNCTIVE | PLUPERFECT SUBJUNCTIVE |
|---|---|---|---|---|---|---|
| he averiguado | hube averiguado | había averiguado | habré averiguado | habría averiguado | haya averiguado | hubiera averiguado |

## 11. -er stem-changing verbs in the present (o → ue) *volver*, devolver, disolver, envolver, llover, mover, resolver, revolver, soler

| PRESENT | PRETERITE | IMPERFECT | CONDITIONAL | FUTURE | PRESENT SUBJUNCTIVE | IMPERFECT SUBJUNCTIVE | IMPERATIVE |
|---|---|---|---|---|---|---|---|
| vuelv o | volv í | volv ía | volver ía | volver é | vuelv a | volvie ra | |
| vuelv es | volv iste | volv ías | volver ías | volver ás | vuelv as | volvie ras | vuelve/no vuelvas |
| vuelv e | volv ió | volv ía | volver ía | volver á | vuelv a | volvie ra | vuelva (Ud.) |
| volv emos | volv imos | volv íamos | volver íamos | volver emos | volv amos | volvié ramos | volvamos |
| volv éis | volv isteis | volv íais | volver íais | volver éis | volv áis | volvie rais | volved/no volváis |
| vuelv en | volv ieron | volv ían | volver ían | volver án | vuelv an | volvie ran | vuelvan |

| PRESENT PERFECT | PAST PERFECT | PLUPERFECT | FUTURE PERFECT | CONDITIONAL PERFECT | PRESENT PERFECT SUBJUNCTIVE | IMPERFECT SUBJUNCTIVE | PLUPERFECT SUBJUNCTIVE |
|---|---|---|---|---|---|---|---|
| he vuelto | hube vuelto | había vuelto | habré vuelto | habría vuelto | haya vuelto | volvie ran | hubiera vuelto |

PPRESENT PERFECT: he vuelto

## 12. -ir stem-changing verbs in the present (o → ue) *dormir*(se), morir(se)

| PRESENT | PRETERITE | IMPERFECT | CONDITIONAL | FUTURE | PRESENT SUBJUNCTIVE | IMPERFECT SUBJUNCTIVE | IMPERATIVE |
|---|---|---|---|---|---|---|---|
| duerm o | dorm í | dorm ía | dormir ía | dormir é | duerm a | durmie ra | |
| duerm es | dorm iste | dorm ías | dormir ías | dormir ás | duerm as | durmie ras | duerme/ no duermas |
| duerm e | durm ió | dorm ía | dormir ía | dormir á | duerm a | durmie ra | duerma (Ud.) |
| dorm imos | dorm imos | dorm íamos | dormir íamos | dormir emos | durm amos | durmié ramos | durmamos |
| dorm is | dorm isteis | dorm íais | dormir íais | dormir éis | durm áis | durmie rais | dormid/no durmáis |
| duerm en | durm ieron | dorm ían | dormir ían | dormir án | duerm an | durmie ran | duerman |

| PRESENT PERFECT | PAST PERFECT | PLUPERFECT | FUTURE PERFECT | CONDITIONAL PERFECT | PRESENT PERFECT SUBJUNCTIVE | PLUPERFECT SUBJUNCTIVE |
|---|---|---|---|---|---|---|
| he dormido | hube dormido | había dormido | habré dormido | habría dormido | haya dormido | hubiera dormido |

## 13. -er stem-changing verbs ending in *a vowel + cer* (c → zc) in front of *a* and *o* *conocer*, agradecer, crecer, establecer, merecer, nacer, obedecer, ofrecer

| PRESENT | PRETERITE | IMPERFECT | CONDITIONAL | FUTURE | PRESENT SUBJUNCTIVE | IMPERFECT SUBJUNCTIVE | IMPERATIVE |
|---|---|---|---|---|---|---|---|
| conozc o | conoc í | conoc ía | conocer ía | conocer é | conozc a | conocie ra | |
| conoc es | conoc iste | conoc ías | conocer ías | conocer ás | conozc as | conocie ras | conoce/no conozcas |
| conoc e | conoc ió | conoc ía | conocer ía | conocer á | conozc a | conocie ra | conozca (Ud.) |
| conoc emos | conoc imos | conoc íamos | conocer íamos | conocer emos | conozc amos | conocié ramos | conozcamos |
| conoc éis | conoc isteis | conoc íais | conocer íais | conocer éis | conozc áis | conocie rais | conoced/no conozcáis |
| conoc en | conoc ieron | conoc ían | conocer ían | conocer án | conozc an | conocie ran | conozcan |

| PRESENT PERFECT | PAST PERFECT | PLUPERFECT | FUTURE PERFECT | CONDITIONAL PERFECT | PRESENT PERFECT SUBJUNCTIVE | PLUPERFECT SUBJUNCTIVE |
|---|---|---|---|---|---|---|
| he conocido | hube conocido | había conocido | habré conocido | habría conocido | haya conocido | hubiera conocido |

## 14. -ir stem-changing verbs ending in *a vowel + cir* (z → zc) in front of *a* and *o*, and (c → j) *conducir*, deducir, introducir, producir, reducir, traducir

| PRESENT | PRETERITE | IMPERFECT | CONDITIONAL | FUTURE | PRESENT SUBJUNCTIVE | IMPERFECT SUBJUNCTIVE | IMPERATIVE |
|---|---|---|---|---|---|---|---|
| conduzc o | conduj e | conduc ía | conducir ía | conducir é | conduzc a | conduje ra | |
| conduc es | conduj iste | conduc ías | conducir ías | conducir ás | conduzc as | conduje ras | conduce/no conduzcas |
| conduc e | conduj o | conduc ía | conducir ía | conducir á | conduzc a | conduje ra | conduzca (Ud.) |
| conduc imos | conduj imos | conduc íamos | conducir íamos | conducir emos | conduzc amos | condujé ramos | conduzcamos |
| conduc is | conduj isteis | conduc íais | conducir íais | conducir éis | conduzc áis | conduje rais | conducid/no conduzcáis |
| conduc en | conduj eron | conduc ían | conducir ían | conducir án | conduzc an | conduje ran | conduzcan |

| PRESENT PERFECT | PAST PERFECT | PLUPERFECT | FUTURE PERFECT | CONDITIONAL PERFECT | PRESENT PERFECT SUBJUNCTIVE | PLUPERFECT SUBJUNCTIVE |
|---|---|---|---|---|---|---|
| he conducido | hube conducido | había conducido | habré conducido | habría conducido | haya conducido | hubiera conducido |

## 15. stem-changing verbs ending in -ger: (g → j) in front of a and o escoger, acoger, coger, encoger, proteger, recoger

| PRESENT | PRETERITE | IMPERFECT | FUTURE | CONDITIONAL | PRESENT SUBJUNCTIVE | IMPERFECT SUBJUNCTIVE | IMPERATIVE |
|---|---|---|---|---|---|---|---|
| escoj o | escog í | escog ía | escoger é | escoger ía | escoj a | escogie ra | |
| escog es | escog iste | escog ías | escoger ás | escoger ías | escoj as | escogie ras | escoge/no escojas |
| escog e | escog ió | escog ía | escoger á | escoger ía | escoj a | escogie ra | escoja (Ud.) |
| escog emos | escog imos | escog íamos | escoger emos | escoger íamos | escoj amos | escogié ramos | escojamos |
| escog éis | escog isteis | escog íais | escoger éis | escoger íais | escoj áis | escogie rais | escoged/no escojáis |
| escog en | escog ieron | escog ían | escoger án | escoger ían | escoj an | escogie ran | escojan |

| PRESENT PERFECT | PAST PERFECT | PLUPERFECT | FUTURE PERFECT | CONDITIONAL PERFECT | PRESENT PERFECT | IMPERFECT SUBJUNCTIVE | PLUPERFECT SUBJUNCTIVE |
|---|---|---|---|---|---|---|---|
| he escogido | hube escogido | había escogido | habré escogido | habría escogido | haya escogido | había escogido | hubiera escogido |

## 16. stem-changing verbs ending in -gir (g → j) in front of a and o; ir: (e → i) elegir, colegir, corregir, reelegir, regir

| PRESENT | PRETERITE | IMPERFECT | FUTURE | CONDITIONAL | PRESENT SUBJUNCTIVE | IMPERFECT SUBJUNCTIVE | IMPERATIVE |
|---|---|---|---|---|---|---|---|
| elij o | eleg í | eleg ía | elegir é | elegir ía | elij a | eligie ra | |
| elig es | eleg iste | eleg ías | elegir ás | elegir ías | elij as | eligie ras | elige/no elijas |
| elig e | elig ió | eleg ía | elegir á | elegir ía | elij a | eligie ra | elija (Ud.) |
| eleg imos | eleg imos | eleg íamos | elegir emos | elegir íamos | elij amos | eligié ramos | elijamos |
| eleg ís | eleg isteis | eleg íais | elegir éis | elegir íais | elij áis | eligie rais | elegid/no elijáis |
| elig en | elig ieron | eleg ían | elegir án | elegir ían | elij an | eligie ran | elijan |

| PRESENT PERFECT | PAST PERFECT | PLUPERFECT | FUTURE PERFECT | CONDITIONAL PERFECT | PRESENT PERFECT | IMPERFECT SUBJUNCTIVE | PLUPERFECT SUBJUNCTIVE |
|---|---|---|---|---|---|---|---|
| he elegido | hube elegido | había elegido | habré elegido | habría elegido | haya elegido | había elegido | hubiera elegido |

## 17. stem-changing verbs ending in -guir (gu → g) in front of a and o; ir: (e → i) seguir, conseguir, perseguir, proseguir

| PRESENT | PRETERITE | IMPERFECT | FUTURE | CONDITIONAL | PRESENT SUBJUNCTIVE | IMPERFECT SUBJUNCTIVE | IMPERATIVE |
|---|---|---|---|---|---|---|---|
| sig o | segu í | segu ía | seguir é | seguir ía | sig a | siguie ra | |
| sigu es | segu iste | segu ías | seguir ás | seguir ías | sig as | siguie ras | sigue/no sigas |
| sigu e | sigu ió | segu ía | seguir á | seguir ía | sig a | siguie ra | siga (Ud.) |
| segu imos | segu imos | segu íamos | seguir emos | seguir íamos | sig amos | siguié ramos | sigamos |
| segu ís | segu isteis | segu íais | seguir éis | seguir íais | sig áis | siguie rais | seguid/no sigáis |
| sigu en | sigu ieron | segu ían | seguir án | seguir ían | sig an | siguie ran | sigan |

| PRESENT PERFECT | PAST PERFECT | PLUPERFECT | FUTURE PERFECT | CONDITIONAL PERFECT | PRESENT PERFECT | IMPERFECT SUBJUNCTIVE | PLUPERFECT SUBJUNCTIVE |
|---|---|---|---|---|---|---|---|
| he seguido | hube seguido | había seguido | habré seguido | habría seguido | haya seguido | había seguido | hubiera seguido |

## 18. stem-changing verbs ending in -zar: (z → c) in front of e cruzar, almorzar (o → ue), bostezar, comenzar (e → ie), empezar (e → ie), reemplazar

| PRESENT | PRETERITE | IMPERFECT | FUTURE | CONDITIONAL | PRESENT SUBJUNCTIVE | IMPERFECT SUBJUNCTIVE | IMPERATIVE |
|---|---|---|---|---|---|---|---|
| cruz o | cruc é | cruz aba | cruzar é | cruzar ía | cruc e | cruza ra | |
| cruz as | cruz aste | cruz abas | cruzar ás | cruzar ías | cruc es | cruza ras | cruza/no cruces |
| cruz a | cruz ó | cruz aba | cruzar á | cruzar ía | cruc e | cruza ra | cruce (Ud.) |
| cruz amos | cruz amos | cruz ábamos | cruzar emos | cruzar íamos | cruc emos | cruzá ramos | crucemos |
| cruz áis | cruz asteis | cruz abais | cruzar éis | cruzar íais | cruc éis | cruza rais | cruzad/no crucéis |
| cruz an | cruz aron | cruz aban | cruzar án | cruzar ían | cruc en | cruza ran | crucen |

| PRESENT PERFECT | PAST PERFECT | PLUPERFECT | FUTURE PERFECT | CONDITIONAL PERFECT | PRESENT PERFECT | IMPERFECT SUBJUNCTIVE | PLUPERFECT SUBJUNCTIVE |
|---|---|---|---|---|---|---|---|
| he cruzado | hube cruzado | había cruzado | habré cruzado | habría cruzado | haya cruzado | había cruzado | hubiera cruzado |

### 19. stem-changing verbs ending in -car (c → qu) in front of e  buscar, acercar, explicar, indicar, justificar, sacar, significar

| PRESENT | PRETERITE | IMPERFECT | FUTURE | CONDITIONAL | PRESENT SUBJUNCTIVE | IMPERFECT SUBJUNCTIVE | IMPERATIVE |
|---|---|---|---|---|---|---|---|
| busc o | busqu é | busc aba | buscar é | buscar ía | busqu e | busca ra | |
| busc as | busc aste | busc abas | buscar ás | buscar ías | busqu es | busca ras | busca/no busques |
| busc a | busc ó | busc aba | buscar á | buscar ía | busqu e | busca ra | busque (Ud.) |
| busc amos | busc amos | busc ábamos | buscar emos | buscar íamos | busqu emos | buscá ramos | busquemos |
| busc áis | busc asteis | busc abais | buscar éis | buscar íais | busqu éis | busca rais | buscad/no busquéis |
| busc an | busc aron | busc aban | buscar án | buscar ían | busqu en | busca ran | busquen |

| PRESENT PERFECT | PAST PERFECT | PLUPERFECT | FUTURE PERFECT | CONDITIONAL PERFECT | PRESENT PERFECT SUBJUNCTIVE | PRESENT PERFECT SUBJUNCTIVE | PLUPERFECT SUBJUNCTIVE |
|---|---|---|---|---|---|---|---|
| he buscado | hube buscado | había buscado | habré buscado | habría buscado | haya buscado | haya buscado | hubiera buscado |

### 20. stem-changing verbs ending in -gar (g → gu) in front of e  llegar, abrigar, vagar, jugar (u → ue)

| PRESENT | PRETERITE | IMPERFECT | FUTURE | CONDITIONAL | PRESENT SUBJUNCTIVE | IMPERFECT SUBJUNCTIVE | IMPERATIVE |
|---|---|---|---|---|---|---|---|
| lleg o | llegu é | lleg aba | llegar é | llegar ía | llegu e | llega ra | |
| lleg as | lleg aste | lleg abas | llegar ás | llegar ías | llegu es | llega ras | llega/no llegues |
| lleg a | lleg ó | lleg aba | llegar á | llegar ía | llegu e | llega ra | llegue (Ud.) |
| lleg amos | lleg amos | lleg ábamos | llegar emos | llegar íamos | llegu emos | llegá ramos | lleguemos |
| lleg áis | lleg asteis | lleg abais | llegar éis | llegar íais | llegu éis | llega rais | llegad/no lleguéis |
| lleg an | lleg aron | lleg aban | llegar án | llegar ían | llegu en | llega ran | lleguen |

| PRESENT PERFECT | PAST PERFECT | PLUPERFECT | FUTURE PERFECT | CONDITIONAL PERFECT | PRESENT PERFECT SUBJUNCTIVE | PLUPERFECT SUBJUNCTIVE |
|---|---|---|---|---|---|---|
| he llegado | hube llegado | había llegado | habré llegado | habría llegado | haya llegado | hubiera llegado |

### 21. stem-changing verbs ending in -iar (i → í)  enviar, ampliar, confiar, enfriar, espiar, guiar, resfriarse, rociar, vaciar, variar

| PRESENT | PRETERITE | IMPERFECT | FUTURE | CONDITIONAL | PRESENT SUBJUNCTIVE | IMPERFECT SUBJUNCTIVE | IMPERATIVE |
|---|---|---|---|---|---|---|---|
| env ío | envi é | envi aba | enviar é | enviar ía | env íe | envia ra | |
| env ías | envi aste | envi abas | enviar ás | enviar ías | env íes | envia ras | envía/no envíes |
| env ía | envi ó | envi aba | enviar á | enviar ía | env íe | envia ra | envíe (Ud.) |
| envi amos | envi amos | envi ábamos | enviar emos | enviar íamos | envi emos | enviá ramos | enviemos |
| envi áis | envi asteis | envi abais | enviar éis | enviar íais | envi éis | envia rais | enviad/no enviéis |
| env ían | envi aron | envi aban | enviar án | enviar ían | env íen | envia ran | envíen |

| PRESENT PERFECT | PAST PERFECT | PLUPERFECT | FUTURE PERFECT | CONDITIONAL PERFECT | PRESENT PERFECT SUBJUNCTIVE | PLUPERFECT SUBJUNCTIVE |
|---|---|---|---|---|---|---|
| he enviado | hube enviado | había enviado | habré enviado | habría enviado | haya enviado | hubiera enviado |

### 22. stem-changing verbs ending in -uar (u → ú)  continuar, acentuar, actuar, evaluar, graduarse, insinuar

| PRESENT | PRETERITE | IMPERFECT | FUTURE | CONDITIONAL | PRESENT SUBJUNCTIVE | IMPERFECT SUBJUNCTIVE | IMPERATIVE |
|---|---|---|---|---|---|---|---|
| continú o | continu é | continu aba | continuar é | continuar ía | continú e | continua ra | |
| continú as | continu aste | continu abas | continuar ás | continuar ías | continú es | continua ras | continúa/no continúes |
| continú a | continu ó | continu aba | continuar á | continuar ía | continú e | continua ra | continúe (Ud.) |
| continu amos | continu amos | continu ábamos | continuar emos | continuar íamos | continu emos | continuá ramos | continuemos |
| continu áis | continu asteis | continu abais | continuar éis | continuar íais | continu éis | continua rais | continuad/no continuéis |
| continú an | continu aron | continu aban | continuar án | continuar ían | continú en | continua ran | continúen |

| PRESENT PERFECT | PAST PERFECT | PLUPERFECT | FUTURE PERFECT | CONDITIONAL PERFECT | PRESENT PERFECT SUBJUNCTIVE | PRESENT PERFECT SUBJUNCTIVE | PLUPERFECT SUBJUNCTIVE |
|---|---|---|---|---|---|---|---|
| he continuado | hube continuado | había continuado | habré continuado | habría continuado | haya continuado | haya continuado | hubiera continuado |

## 23. stem-changing verbs ending in -uir (i → y) *destruir*, atribuir, construir, contribuir, disminuir, distribuir, huir, incluir, influir, obstruir, sustituir

| PRESENT | PRETERITE | IMPERFECT | FUTURE | CONDITIONAL | PRESENT SUBJUNCTIVE | IMPERFECT SUBJUNCTIVE | IMPERATIVE |
|---|---|---|---|---|---|---|---|
| destruyo | destruí | destruía | destruiré | destruiría | destruya | destruyera | |
| destruyes | destruiste | destruías | destruirás | destruirías | destruyas | destruyeras | destruye/no destruyas |
| destruye | destruyó | destruía | destruirá | destruiría | destruya | destruyera | destruya (Ud.) |
| destruimos | destruimos | destruíamos | destruiremos | destruiríamos | destruyamos | destruyéramos | destruyamos |
| destruís | destruisteis | destruíais | destruiréis | destruiríais | destruyáis | destruyerais | destruid/no destruyáis |
| destruyen | destruyeron | destruían | destruirán | destruirían | destruyan | destruyeran | destruyan |

| PRESENT PERFECT | PAST PERFECT | PLUPERFECT | FUTURE PERFECT | CONDITIONAL PERFECT | PRESENT PERFECT SUBJUNCTIVE | PLUPERFECT SUBJUNCTIVE |
|---|---|---|---|---|---|---|
| he destruido | hube destruido | había destruido | habré destruido | habría destruido | haya destruido | hubiera destruido |

## IRREGULAR VERBS

### 24. Infinitive: andar    Present participle (gerund): andando    Past participle: andado

| PRESENT | PRETERITE | IMPERFECT | FUTURE | CONDITIONAL | PRESENT SUBJUNCTIVE | IMPERFECT SUBJUNCTIVE | IMPERATIVE |
|---|---|---|---|---|---|---|---|
| ando | anduve | andaba | andaré | andaría | ande | anduviera | |
| andas | anduviste | andabas | andarás | andarías | andes | anduvieras | anda/no andes |
| anda | anduvo | andaba | andará | andaría | ande | anduviera | ande (Ud.) |
| andamos | anduvimos | andábamos | andaremos | andaríamos | andemos | anduviéramos | andemos |
| andáis | anduvisteis | andabais | andaréis | andaríais | andéis | anduvierais | andad/no andéis |
| andan | anduvieron | andaban | andarán | andarían | anden | anduvieran | anden |

| PRESENT PERFECT | PAST PERFECT | PLUPERFECT | FUTURE PERFECT | CONDITIONAL PERFECT | PRESENT PERFECT SUBJUNCTIVE | PLUPERFECT SUBJUNCTIVE |
|---|---|---|---|---|---|---|
| he andado | hube andado | había andado | habré andado | habría andado | haya andado | hubiera andado |

### 25. Infinitive: caber    Present participle (gerund): cabiendo    Past participle: cabido

| PRESENT | PRETERITE | IMPERFECT | FUTURE | CONDITIONAL | PRESENT SUBJUNCTIVE | IMPERFECT SUBJUNCTIVE | IMPERATIVE |
|---|---|---|---|---|---|---|---|
| quepo | cupe | cabía | cabré | cabría | quepa | cupiera | |
| cabes | cupiste | cabías | cabrás | cabrías | quepas | cupieras | cabe/no quepas |
| cabe | cupo | cabía | cabrá | cabría | quepa | cupiera | quepa (Ud.) |
| cabemos | cupimos | cabíamos | cabremos | cabríamos | quepamos | cupiéramos | quepamos |
| cabéis | cupisteis | cabíais | cabréis | cabríais | quepáis | cupierais | cabed/no quepáis |
| caben | cupieron | cabían | cabrán | cabrían | quepan | cupieran | quepan |

| PRESENT PERFECT | PAST PERFECT | PLUPERFECT | FUTURE PERFECT | CONDITIONAL PERFECT | PRESENT PERFECT SUBJUNCTIVE | PLUPERFECT SUBJUNCTIVE |
|---|---|---|---|---|---|---|
| he cabido | hube cabido | había cabido | habré cabido | habría cabido | haya cabido | hubiera cabido |

**Compound tenses:** they are formed with the correspondent tenses of **haber + past participle**

## 26. Infinitive: caer   Present participle (gerund): cayendo   Past participle: caído   de/re caer

| PRESENT | PRETERITE | IMPERFECT | FUTURE | CONDITIONAL | PRESENT SUBJUNCTIVE | IMPERFECT SUBJUNCTIVE | IMPERATIVE |
|---|---|---|---|---|---|---|---|
| caigo | caí | caía | caeré | caería | caiga | cayera | |
| caes | caíste | caías | caerás | caerías | caigas | cayeras | cae/no caigas |
| cae | cayó | caía | caerá | caería | caiga | cayera | caiga (Ud.) |
| caemos | caímos | caíamos | caeremos | caeríamos | caigamos | cayéramos | caigamos |
| caéis | caísteis | caíais | caeréis | caeríais | caigáis | cayerais | caed/no caigáis |
| caen | cayeron | caían | caerán | caerían | caigan | cayeran | caigan |

| PRESENT PERFECT | PAST PERFECT | PLUPERFECT | FUTURE PERFECT | CONDITIONAL PERFECT | PRESENT PERFECT SUBJUNCTIVE | PLUPERFECT SUBJUNCTIVE |
|---|---|---|---|---|---|---|
| he caído | hube caído | había caído | habré caído | habría caído | haya caído | hubiera caído |

## 27. Infinitive: creer   Present participle (gerund): creyendo   Past participle: creído

| PRESENT | PRETERITE | IMPERFECT | FUTURE | CONDITIONAL | PRESENT SUBJUNCTIVE | IMPERFECT SUBJUNCTIVE | IMPERATIVE |
|---|---|---|---|---|---|---|---|
| creo | creí | creía | creeré | creería | crea | creyera | |
| crees | creíste | creías | creerás | creerías | creas | creyeras | cree/no creas |
| cree | creyó | creía | creerá | creería | crea | creyera | crea (Ud.) |
| creemos | creímos | creíamos | creeremos | creeríamos | creamos | creyéramos | creamos |
| creéis | creísteis | creíais | creeréis | creeríais | creáis | creyerais | creed/no creáis |
| creen | creyeron | creían | creerán | creerían | crean | creyeran | crean |

| PRESENT PERFECT | PAST PERFECT | PLUPERFECT | FUTURE PERFECT | CONDITIONAL PERFECT | PRESENT PERFECT SUBJUNCTIVE | PLUPERFECT SUBJUNCTIVE |
|---|---|---|---|---|---|---|
| he creído | hube creído | había creído | habré creído | habría creído | haya creído | hubiera creído |

## 28. Infinitive: dar   Present participle (gerund): dando   Past participle: dado

| PRESENT | PRETERITE | IMPERFECT | FUTURE | CONDITIONAL | PRESENT SUBJUNCTIVE | IMPERFECT SUBJUNCTIVE | IMPERATIVE |
|---|---|---|---|---|---|---|---|
| doy | di | daba | daré | daría | dé | die **ra** | |
| das | diste | dabas | darás | darías | des | die **ras** | da/no des |
| da | dio | daba | dará | daría | dé | die **ra** | dé (Ud.) |
| damos | dimos | dábamos | daremos | daríamos | demos | dié **ramos** | demos |
| dais | disteis | dabais | daréis | daríais | deis | die **rais** | dad/no deis |
| dan | dieron | daban | darán | darían | den | die **ran** | den |

| PRESENT PERFECT | PAST PERFECT | PLUPERFECT | FUTURE PERFECT | CONDITIONAL PERFECT | PRESENT PERFECT SUBJUNCTIVE | PLUPERFECT SUBJUNCTIVE |
|---|---|---|---|---|---|---|
| **he** dado | **hube** dado | **había** dado | **habré** dado | **habría** dado | **haya** dado | **hubiera** dado |

## 29. Infinitive: decir   Present participle (gerund): diciendo   Past participle: dicho

| PRESENT | PRETERITE | IMPERFECT | FUTURE | CONDITIONAL | PRESENT SUBJUNCTIVE | IMPERFECT SUBJUNCTIVE | IMPERATIVE |
|---|---|---|---|---|---|---|---|
| digo | dije | decía | diré | diría | diga | dijera | |
| dices | dijiste | decías | dirás | dirías | digas | dijeras | di/no digas |
| dice | dijo | decía | dirá | diría | diga | dijera | diga (Ud.) |
| decimos | dijimos | decíamos | diremos | diríamos | digamos | dijéramos | digamos |
| decís | dijisteis | decíais | diréis | diríais | digáis | dijerais | decid/no digáis |
| dicen | dijeron | decían | dirán | dirían | digan | dijeran | digan |

| PRESENT PERFECT | PAST PERFECT | PLUPERFECT | FUTURE PERFECT | CONDITIONAL PERFECT | PRESENT PERFECT SUBJUNCTIVE | PLUPERFECT SUBJUNCTIVE |
|---|---|---|---|---|---|---|
| **he** dicho | **hube** dicho | **había** dicho | **habré** dicho | **habría** dicho | **haya** dicho | **hubiera** dicho |

## 30. Infinitive: estar    Present participle (gerund): estando    Past participle: estado

| PRESENT | PRETERITE | IMPERFECT | FUTURE | CONDITIONAL | PRESENT SUBJUNCTIVE | IMPERFECT SUBJUNCTIVE | IMPERATIVE |
|---|---|---|---|---|---|---|---|
| estoy | estuve | estaba | estaré | estaría | esté | estuviera | está/no estés |
| estás | estuviste | estabas | estarás | estarías | estés | estuvieras | esté (Ud.) |
| está | estuvo | estaba | estará | estaría | esté | estuviera | estemos |
| estamos | estuvimos | estábamos | estaremos | estaríamos | estemos | estuviéramos | estad/no estéis |
| estáis | estuvisteis | estabais | estaréis | estaríais | estéis | estuvierais | estén |
| están | estuvieron | estaban | estarán | estarían | estén | estuvieran | |

| PRESENT PERFECT | PAST PERFECT | PLUPERFECT | FUTURE PERFECT | CONDITIONAL PERFECT | PRESENT PERFECT SUBJUNCTIVE | PLUPERFECT SUBJUNCTIVE |
|---|---|---|---|---|---|---|
| **he** estado | **hube** estado | **había** estado | **habré** estado | **habría** estado | **haya** estado | **hubiera** estado |

## 31. Infinitive: haber    Present participle (gerund): habiendo    Past participle: habido

| PRESENT | PRETERITE | IMPERFECT | FUTURE | CONDITIONAL | PRESENT SUBJUNCTIVE | IMPERFECT SUBJUNCTIVE |
|---|---|---|---|---|---|---|
| he | hube | había | habré | habría | haya | hubiera |
| has | hubiste | habías | habrás | habrías | hayas | hubieras |
| ha | hubo | había | habrá | habría | haya | hubiera |
| hemos | hubimos | habíamos | habremos | habríamos | hayamos | hubiéramos |
| habéis | hubisteis | habíais | habréis | habríais | hayáis | hubierais |
| han | hubieron | habían | habrán | habrían | hayan | hubieran |

| PRESENT PERFECT | PAST PERFECT | PLUPERFECT | FUTURE PERFECT | CONDITIONAL PERFECT | PRESENT PERFECT SUBJUNCTIVE | PLUPERFECT SUBJUNCTIVE |
|---|---|---|---|---|---|---|
| **he** habido | **hube** habido | **había** habido | **habré** habido | **habría** habido | **haya** habido | **hubiera** habido |

## 32. Infinitive: hacer    Present participle (gerund): haciendo    Past participle: hecho des/rehacer

| PRESENT | PRETERITE | IMPERFECT | FUTURE | CONDITIONAL | PRESENT SUBJUNCTIVE | IMPERFECT SUBJUNCTIVE | IMPERATIVE |
|---|---|---|---|---|---|---|---|
| hago | hice | hacía | haré | haría | haga | hiciera | haz/no hagas |
| haces | hiciste | hacías | harás | harías | hagas | hicieras | haga (Ud.) |
| hace | hizo | hacía | hará | haría | haga | hiciera | hagamos |
| hacemos | hicimos | hacíamos | haremos | haríamos | hagamos | hiciéramos | haced/no hagáis |
| hacéis | hicisteis | hacíais | haréis | haríais | hagáis | hicierais | hagan |
| hacen | hicieron | hacían | harán | harían | hagan | hicieran | |

| PRESENT PERFECT | PAST PERFECT | PLUPERFECT | FUTURE PERFECT | CONDITIONAL PERFECT | PRESENT PERFECT SUBJUNCTIVE | PLUPERFECT SUBJUNCTIVE |
|---|---|---|---|---|---|---|
| **he** hecho | **hube** hecho | **había** hecho | **habré** hecho | **habría** hecho | **haya** hecho | **hubiera** hecho |

## 33. Infinitive: ir    Present participle (gerund): yendo    Past participle: ido

| PRESENT | PRETERITE | IMPERFECT | FUTURE | CONDITIONAL | PRESENT SUBJUNCTIVE | IMPERFECT SUBJUNCTIVE | IMPERATIVE |
|---|---|---|---|---|---|---|---|
| voy | fui | iba | iré | iría | vaya | fuera | ve/no vayas |
| vas | fuiste | ibas | irás | irías | vayas | fueras | vaya (Ud.) |
| va | fue | iba | irá | iría | vaya | fuera | vamos/no vayamos |
| vamos | fuimos | íbamos | iremos | iríamos | vayamos | fuéramos | id/no vayáis |
| vais | fuisteis | ibais | iréis | iríais | vayáis | fuerais | vayan |
| van | fueron | iban | irán | irían | vayan | fueran | |

| PRESENT PERFECT | PAST PERFECT | PLUPERFECT | FUTURE PERFECT | CONDITIONAL PERFECT | PRESENT PERFECT SUBJUNCTIVE | PLUPERFECT SUBJUNCTIVE |
|---|---|---|---|---|---|---|
| **he** ido | **hube** ido | **había** ido | **habré** ido | **habría** ido | **haya** ido | **hubiera** ido |

## 34. Infinitive: **leer**  Present participle (gerund): leyendo  Past participle: leído

| PRESENT | PRETERITE | IMPERFECT | FUTURE | CONDITIONAL | PRESENT SUBJUNCTIVE | IMPERFECT SUBJUNCTIVE | IMPERATIVE |
|---|---|---|---|---|---|---|---|
| leo | leí | leía | leeré | leería | lea | leyera | |
| lees | leíste | leías | leerás | leerías | leas | leyeras | lee/no leas |
| lee | leyó | leía | leerá | leería | lea | leyera | lea (Ud.) |
| leemos | leímos | leíamos | leeremos | leeríamos | leamos | leyéramos | leamos |
| leéis | leísteis | leíais | leeréis | leeríais | leáis | leyerais | leed/no leáis |
| leen | leyeron | leían | leerán | leerían | lean | leyeran | lean |

| PRESENT PERFECT | PAST PERFECT | PLUPERFECT | FUTURE PERFECT | CONDITIONAL PERFECT | PRESENT PERFECT SUBJUNCTIVE | PLUPERFECT SUBJUNCTIVE |
|---|---|---|---|---|---|---|
| **he** leído | **hube** leído | **había** leído | **habré** leído | **habría** leído | **haya** leído | **hubiera** leído |

## 35. Infinitive: **oír**  Present participle (gerund): oyendo  Past participle: oído

| PRESENT | PRETERITE | IMPERFECT | FUTURE | CONDITIONAL | PRESENT SUBJUNCTIVE | IMPERFECT SUBJUNCTIVE | IMPERATIVE |
|---|---|---|---|---|---|---|---|
| oigo | oí | oía | oiré | oiría | oiga | oyera | |
| oyes | oíste | oías | oirás | oirías | oigas | oyeras | oye/no oigas |
| oye | oyó | oía | oirá | oiría | oiga | oyera | oiga (Ud.) |
| oímos | oímos | oíamos | oiremos | oiríamos | oigamos | oyéramos | oigamos |
| oís | oísteis | oíais | oiréis | oiríais | oigáis | oyerais | oíd/no oigáis |
| oyen | oyeron | oían | oirán | oirían | oigan | oyeran | oigan |

| PRESENT PERFECT | PAST PERFECT | PLUPERFECT | FUTURE PERFECT | CONDITIONAL PERFECT | PRESENT PERFECT SUBJUNCTIVE | PLUPERFECT SUBJUNCTIVE |
|---|---|---|---|---|---|---|
| **he** oído | **hube** oído | **había** oído | **habré** oído | **habría** oído | **haya** oído | **hubiera** oído |

## 36. Infinitive: **oler**  Present participle (gerund): oliendo  Past participle: olido

| PRESENT | PRETERITE | IMPERFECT | FUTURE | CONDITIONAL | PRESENT SUBJUNCTIVE | IMPERFECT SUBJUNCTIVE | IMPERATIVE |
|---|---|---|---|---|---|---|---|
| huelo | olí | olía | oleré | olería | huela | oliera | |
| hueles | oliste | olías | olerás | olerías | huelas | olieras | huele/no huelas |
| huele | olió | olía | olerá | olería | huela | oliera | huela (Ud.) |
| olemos | olimos | olíamos | oleremos | oleríamos | olamos | oliéramos | olamos |
| oléis | olisteis | olíais | oleréis | oleríais | oláis | olierais | oled/no oláis |
| huelen | olieron | olían | olerán | olerían | huelan | olieran | huelan |

| PRESENT PERFECT | PAST PERFECT | PLUPERFECT | FUTURE PERFECT | CONDITIONAL PERFECT | PRESENT PERFECT SUBJUNCTIVE | PLUPERFECT SUBJUNCTIVE |
|---|---|---|---|---|---|---|
| **he** olido | **hube** olido | **había** olido | **habré** olido | **habría** olido | **haya** olido | **hubiera** olido |

## 37. Infinitive: **poder**  Present participle (gerund): pudiendo  Past participle: podido

| PRESENT | PRETERITE | IMPERFECT | FUTURE | CONDITIONAL | PRESENT SUBJUNCTIVE | IMPERFECT SUBJUNCTIVE |
|---|---|---|---|---|---|---|
| puedo | pude | podía | podré | podría | pueda | pudiera |
| puedes | pudiste | podías | podrás | podrías | puedas | pudieras |
| puede | pudo | podía | podrá | podría | pueda | pudiera |
| podemos | pudimos | podíamos | podremos | podríamos | podamos | pudiéramos |
| podéis | pudisteis | podíais | podréis | podríais | podáis | pudierais |
| pueden | pudieron | podían | podrán | podrían | puedan | pudieran |

| PRESENT PERFECT | PAST PERFECT | PLUPERFECT | FUTURE PERFECT | CONDITIONAL PERFECT | PRESENT PERFECT SUBJUNCTIVE | PLUPERFECT SUBJUNCTIVE |
|---|---|---|---|---|---|---|
| **he** podido | **hube** podido | **había** podido | **habré** podido | **habría** podido | **haya** podido | **hubiera** podido |

## 38. Infinitive: poner    Present participle (gerund): poniendo    Past participle: puesto

| PRESENT | PRETERITE | IMPERFECT | FUTURE | CONDITIONAL | PRESENT SUBJUNCTIVE | IMPERFECT SUBJUNCTIVE | IMPERATIVE |
|---|---|---|---|---|---|---|---|
| pongo | puse | ponía | pondré | pondría | ponga | pusiera | |
| pones | pusiste | ponías | pondrás | pondrías | pongas | pusieras | pon/no pongas |
| pone | puso | ponía | pondrá | pondría | ponga | pusiera | ponga (Ud.) |
| ponemos | pusimos | poníamos | pondremos | pondríamos | pongamos | pusiéramos | pongamos |
| ponéis | pusisteis | poníais | pondréis | pondríais | pongáis | pusierais | poned/no pongáis |
| ponen | pusieron | ponían | pondrán | pondrían | pongan | pusieran | pongan |

| PRESENT PERFECT | PAST PERFECT | PLUPERFECT | FUTURE PERFECT | CONDITIONAL PERFECT | PRESENT PERFECT SUBJUNCTIVE | PLUPERFECT SUBJUNCTIVE |
|---|---|---|---|---|---|---|
| he puesto | hube puesto | había puesto | habré puesto | habría puesto | haya puesto | hubiera puesto |

## 39. Infinitive: prever    Present participle (gerund): previendo    Past participle: previsto

| PRESENT | PRETERITE | IMPERFECT | FUTURE | CONDITIONAL | PRESENT SUBJUNCTIVE | IMPERFECT SUBJUNCTIVE | IMPERATIVE |
|---|---|---|---|---|---|---|---|
| preveo | preví | preveía | preveré | prevería | prevea | previera | |
| prevés | previste | preveías | preverás | preverías | preveas | previeras | prevé/no preveas |
| prevé | previó | preveía | preverá | prevería | prevea | previera | prevea (Ud.) |
| prevemos | previmos | preveíamos | preveremos | preveríamos | preveamos | previéramos | preveamos |
| prevéis | previsteis | preveíais | preveréis | preveríais | preveáis | previerais | preved/no preveáis |
| prevén | previeron | preveían | preverán | preverían | prevean | previeran | prevean |

| PRESENT PERFECT | PAST PERFECT | PLUPERFECT | FUTURE PERFECT | CONDITIONAL PERFECT | PRESENT PERFECT SUBJUNCTIVE | PLUPERFECT SUBJUNCTIVE |
|---|---|---|---|---|---|---|
| he previsto | hube previsto | había previsto | habré previsto | habría previsto | haya previsto | hubiera previsto |

## 40. Infinitive: querer    Present participle (gerund): queriendo    Past participle: querido

| PRESENT | PRETERITE | IMPERFECT | FUTURE | CONDITIONAL | PRESENT SUBJUNCTIVE | IMPERFECT SUBJUNCTIVE | IMPERATIVE |
|---|---|---|---|---|---|---|---|
| quiero | quise | quería | querré | querría | quiera | quisiera | |
| quieres | quisiste | querías | querrás | querrías | quieras | quisieras | quiere/no quieras |
| quiere | quiso | quería | querrá | querría | quiera | quisiera | quiera (Ud.) |
| queremos | quisimos | queríamos | querremos | querríamos | queramos | quisiéramos | queramos |
| queréis | quisisteis | queríais | querréis | querríais | queráis | quisierais | quered/ no queráis |
| quieren | quisieron | querían | querrán | querrían | quieran | quisieran | quieran |

| PRESENT PERFECT | PAST PERFECT | PLUPERFECT | FUTURE PERFECT | CONDITIONAL PERFECT | PRESENT PERFECT SUBJUNCTIVE | PLUPERFECT SUBJUNCTIVE |
|---|---|---|---|---|---|---|
| he querido | hube querido | había querido | habré querido | habría querido | haya querido | hubiera querido |

## 41. Infinitive: reír    Present participle (gerund): riendo    Past participle: reído

| PRESENT | PRETERITE | IMPERFECT | FUTURE | CONDITIONAL | PRESENT SUBJUNCTIVE | IMPERFECT SUBJUNCTIVE | IMPERATIVE |
|---|---|---|---|---|---|---|---|
| río | reí | reía | reiré | reiría | ría | riera | |
| ríes | reíste | reías | reirás | reirías | rías | rieras | ríe/no rías |
| ríe | rió | reía | reirá | reiría | ría | riera | ría (Ud.) |
| reímos | reímos | reíamos | reiremos | reiríamos | riamos | riéramos | riamos |
| reís | reísteis | reíais | reiréis | reiríais | riáis | rierais | reíd/no riáis |
| ríen | rieron | reían | reirán | reirían | rían | rieran | rían |

| PRESENT PERFECT | PAST PERFECT | PLUPERFECT | FUTURE PERFECT | CONDITIONAL PERFECT | PRESENT PERFECT SUBJUNCTIVE | PLUPERFECT SUBJUNCTIVE |
|---|---|---|---|---|---|---|
| he reído | hube reído | había reído | habré reído | habría reído | haya reído | hubiera reído |

## 42. Infinitive: saber    Present participle (gerund): sabiendo    Past participle: sabido

| PRESENT | PRETERITE | IMPERFECT | FUTURE | CONDITIONAL | PRESENT SUBJUNCTIVE | IMPERFECT SUBJUNCTIVE | IMPERATIVE |
|---|---|---|---|---|---|---|---|
| sé | supe | sabía | sabré | sabría | sepa | supiera | |
| sabes | supiste | sabías | sabrás | sabrías | sepas | supieras | sabe/no sepas |
| sabe | supo | sabía | sabrá | sabría | sepa | supiera | sepa (Ud.) |
| sabemos | supimos | sabíamos | sabremos | sabríamos | sepamos | supiéramos | sepamos |
| sabéis | supisteis | sabíais | sabréis | sabríais | sepáis | supierais | sabed/no sepáis |
| saben | supieron | sabían | sabrán | sabrían | sepan | supieran | sepan |

| PRESENT PERFECT | PAST PERFECT | PLUPERFECT | FUTURE PERFECT | CONDITIONAL PERFECT | PRESENT PERFECT SUBJUNCTIVE | PLUPERFECT SUBJUNCTIVE |
|---|---|---|---|---|---|---|
| **he** sabido | **hube** sabido | **había** sabido | **habré** sabido | **habría** sabido | **haya** sabido | **hubiera** sabido |

## 43. Infinitive: salir    Present participle (gerund): saliendo    Past participle: salido

| PRESENT | PRETERITE | IMPERFECT | FUTURE | CONDITIONAL | PRESENT SUBJUNCTIVE | IMPERFECT SUBJUNCTIVE | IMPERATIVE |
|---|---|---|---|---|---|---|---|
| salgo | salí | salía | saldré | saldría | salga | saliera | |
| sales | saliste | salías | saldrás | saldrías | salgas | salieras | sal/no salgas |
| sale | salió | salía | saldrá | saldría | salga | saliera | salga (Ud.) |
| salimos | salimos | salíamos | saldremos | saldríamos | salgamos | saliéramos | salgamos |
| salís | salisteis | salíais | saldréis | saldríais | salgáis | salierais | salid/no salgáis |
| salen | salieron | salían | saldrán | saldrían | salgan | salieran | salgan |

| PRESENT PERFECT | PAST PERFECT | PLUPERFECT | FUTURE PERFECT | CONDITIONAL PERFECT | PRESENT PERFECT SUBJUNCTIVE | PLUPERFECT SUBJUNCTIVE |
|---|---|---|---|---|---|---|
| **he** salido | **hube** salido | **había** salido | **habré** salido | **habría** salido | **haya** salido | **hubiera** salido |

## 44. Infinitive: ser    Present participle (gerund): siendo    Past participle: sido

| PRESENT | PRETERITE | IMPERFECT | FUTURE | CONDITIONAL | PRESENT SUBJUNCTIVE | IMPERFECT SUBJUNCTIVE | IMPERATIVE |
|---|---|---|---|---|---|---|---|
| soy | fui | era | seré | sería | sea | fuera | |
| eres | fuiste | eras | serás | serías | seas | fueras | sé/no seas |
| es | fue | era | será | sería | sea | fuera | sea (Ud.) |
| somos | fuimos | éramos | seremos | seríamos | seamos | fuéramos | seamos |
| sois | fuisteis | erais | seréis | seríais | seáis | fuerais | sed/no seáis |
| son | fueron | eran | serán | serían | sean | fueran | sean |

| PRESENT PERFECT | PAST PERFECT | PLUPERFECT | FUTURE PERFECT | CONDITIONAL PERFECT | PRESENT PERFECT SUBJUNCTIVE | PLUPERFECT SUBJUNCTIVE |
|---|---|---|---|---|---|---|
| **he** sido | **hube** sido | **había** sido | **habré** sido | **habría** sido | **haya** sido | **hubiera** sido |

## 45. Infinitive: tener; con/de/man/ob/re/sostener    Present participle (gerund): teniendo    Past participle: tenido

| PRESENT | PRETERITE | IMPERFECT | FUTURE | CONDITIONAL | PRESENT SUBJUNCTIVE | IMPERFECT SUBJUNCTIVE | IMPERATIVE |
|---|---|---|---|---|---|---|---|
| tengo | tuve | tenía | tendré | tendría | tenga | tuviera | |
| tienes | tuviste | tenías | tendrás | tendrías | tengas | tuvieras | ten/no tengas |
| tiene | tuvo | tenía | tendrá | tendría | tenga | tuviera | tenga (Ud.) |
| tenemos | tuvimos | teníamos | tendremos | tendríamos | tengamos | tuviéramos | tengamos |
| tenéis | tuvisteis | teníais | tendréis | tendríais | tengáis | tuvierais | tened/no tengáis |
| tienen | tuvieron | tenían | tendrán | tendrían | tengan | tuvieran | tengan |

| PRESENT PERFECT | PAST PERFECT | PLUPERFECT | FUTURE PERFECT | CONDITIONAL PERFECT | PRESENT PERFECT SUBJUNCTIVE | PLUPERFECT SUBJUNCTIVE |
|---|---|---|---|---|---|---|
| **he** tenido | **hube** tenido | **había** tenido | **habré** tenido | **habría** tenido | **haya** tenido | **hubiera** tenido |

## 46. Infinitive: **traer**; a/con/dis/ex/retraer

Present participle (gerund): trayendo  Past participle: traído

| PRESENT | PRETERITE | IMPERFECT | FUTURE | CONDITIONAL | PRESENT SUBJUNCTIVE | IMPERFECT SUBJUNCTIVE | IMPERATIVE |
|---|---|---|---|---|---|---|---|
| traigo | traje | traía | traeré | traería | traiga | trajera | |
| traes | trajiste | traías | traerás | traerías | traigas | trajeras | trae/no traigas |
| trae | trajo | traía | traerá | traería | traiga | trajera | traiga (Ud.) |
| traemos | trajimos | traíamos | traeremos | traeríamos | traigamos | trajéramos | traigamos |
| traéis | trajisteis | traíais | traeréis | traeríais | traigáis | trajerais | traed/no traigáis |
| traen | trajeron | traían | traerán | traerían | traigan | trajeran | traigan |

| PRESENT PERFECT | PAST PERFECT | PLUPERFECT | FUTURE PERFECT | CONDITIONAL PERFECT | PRESENT PERFECT SUBJUNCTIVE | PLUPERFECT SUBJUNCTIVE |
|---|---|---|---|---|---|---|
| he traído | hube traído | había traído | habré traído | habría traído | haya traído | hubiera traído |

## 47. Infinitive: **valer**; equivaler

Present participle (gerund): valiendo  Past participle: valido

| PRESENT | PRETERITE | IMPERFECT | FUTURE | CONDITIONAL | PRESENT SUBJUNCTIVE | IMPERFECT SUBJUNCTIVE | IMPERATIVE |
|---|---|---|---|---|---|---|---|
| valgo | valí | valía | valdré | valdría | valga | valiera | |
| vales | valiste | valías | valdrás | valdrías | valgas | valieras | val/no valgas |
| vale | valió | valía | valdrá | valdría | valga | valiera | valga (Ud.) |
| valemos | valimos | valíamos | valdremos | valdríamos | valgamos | valiéramos | valgamos |
| valéis | valisteis | valíais | valdréis | valdríais | valgáis | valierais | valed/no valgáis |
| valen | valieron | valían | valdrán | valdrían | valgan | valieran | valgan |

| PRESENT PERFECT | PAST PERFECT | PLUPERFECT | FUTURE PERFECT | CONDITIONAL PERFECT | PRESENT PERFECT SUBJUNCTIVE | PLUPERFECT SUBJUNCTIVE |
|---|---|---|---|---|---|---|
| he valido | hube valido | había valido | habré valido | habría valido | haya valido | hubiera valido |

## 48. Infinitive: **venir**; con/inter/pre/provenir

Present participle (gerund): viniendo  Past participle: venido

| PRESENT | PRETERITE | IMPERFECT | FUTURE | CONDITIONAL | PRESENT SUBJUNCTIVE | IMPERFECT SUBJUNCTIVE | IMPERATIVE |
|---|---|---|---|---|---|---|---|
| vengo | vine | venía | vendré | vendría | venga | viniera | |
| vienes | viniste | venías | vendrás | vendrías | vengas | vinieras | ven/no vengas |
| viene | vino | venía | vendrá | vendría | venga | viniera | venga (Ud.) |
| venimos | vinimos | veníamos | vendremos | vendríamos | vengamos | viniéramos | vengamos |
| venís | vinisteis | veníais | vendréis | vendríais | vengáis | vinierais | venid/no vengáis |
| vienen | vinieron | venían | vendrán | vendrían | vengan | vinieran | vengan |

| PRESENT PERFECT | PAST PERFECT | PLUPERFECT | FUTURE PERFECT | CONDITIONAL PERFECT | PRESENT PERFECT SUBJUNCTIVE | PLUPERFECT SUBJUNCTIVE |
|---|---|---|---|---|---|---|
| he venido | hube venido | había venido | habré venido | habría venido | haya venido | hubiera venido |

## 49. Infinitive: **ver**

Present participle (gerund): viendo  Past participle: visto

| PRESENT | PRETERITE | IMPERFECT | FUTURE | CONDITIONAL | PRESENT SUBJUNCTIVE | IMPERFECT SUBJUNCTIVE | IMPERATIVE |
|---|---|---|---|---|---|---|---|
| veo | vi | veía | veré | vería | vea | viera | |
| ves | viste | veías | verás | verías | veas | vieras | ve/no veas |
| ve | vio | veía | verá | vería | vea | viera | vea (Ud.) |
| vemos | vimos | veíamos | veremos | veríamos | veamos | viéramos | veamos |
| veis | visteis | veíais | veréis | veríais | veáis | vierais | ved/no veáis |
| ven | vieron | veían | verán | verían | vean | vieran | |

| PRESENT PERFECT | PAST PERFECT | PLUPERFECT | FUTURE PERFECT | CONDITIONAL PERFECT | PRESENT PERFECT SUBJUNCTIVE | PLUPERFECT SUBJUNCTIVE |
|---|---|---|---|---|---|---|
| he visto | hube visto | había visto | habré visto | habría visto | haya visto | hubiera visto |

## 50. -ar verbs: Infinitive: lavarse    Present participle (gerund): lavándose    Past participle: lavado

lavarse, acostarse (o → ue), alegrarse, apurarse, asustarse, callarse, cansarse, casarse, cortarse, despertarse (e → ie), ducharse, enfermarse, enojarse, lastimarse, levantarse, maquillarse, peinarse, resfriarse, secarse

| PRESENT | PRETERITE | IMPERFECT | FUTURE | CONDITIONAL | PRESENT SUBJUNCTIVE | IMPERFECT SUBJUNCTIVE | IMPERATIVE |
|---|---|---|---|---|---|---|---|
| me lavo | me lavé | me lavaba | me lavaré | me lavaría | me lave | me lavara | |
| te lavas | te lavaste | te lavabas | te lavarás | te lavarías | te laves | te lavaras | lávate/no te laves |
| se lava | se lavó | se lavaba | se lavará | se lavaría | se lave | se lavara | lávese (Ud.) |
| nos lavamos | nos lavamos | nos lavábamos | nos lavaremos | nos lavaríamos | nos lavemos | nos lavá ramos | lavémonos |
| os laváis | os lavasteis | os lavabais | os lavaréis | os lavaríais | os lavéis | os lavarais | laváos /no os lavéis |
| se lavan | se lavaron | se lavaban | se lavarán | se lavarían | se laven | se lavaran | lávense |

## 51. -er verbs: Infinitive: ofenderse    Present participle (gerund): ofendiéndose    Past participle: ofendido

ofenderse, caerse, entristecerse (c → zc), romperse, sorprenderse, torcerse (o → ue)

| PRESENT | PRETERITE | IMPERFECT | FUTURE | CONDITIONAL | PRESENT SUBJUNCTIVE | IMPERFECT SUBJUNCTIVE | IMPERATIVE |
|---|---|---|---|---|---|---|---|
| me ofendo | me ofendí | me ofendía | me ofenderé | me ofendería | me ofenda | me ofendiera | |
| te ofendes | te ofendiste | te ofendías | te ofenderás | te ofenderías | te ofendas | te ofendieras | oféndete /no te ofendas |
| se ofende | se ofendió | se ofendía | se ofenderá | se ofendería | se ofenda | se ofendiera | oféndase (Ud.) |
| nos ofendemos | nos ofendimos | nos ofendíamos | nos ofenderemos | nos ofenderíamos | nos ofendamos | nos ofendiéramos | ofendámonos |
| os ofendéis | os ofendisteis | os ofendíais | os ofenderéis | os ofenderíais | os ofendáis | os ofendierais | ofendeos |
| se ofenden | se ofendieron | se ofendían | se ofenderán | se ofenderían | se ofendan | se ofendieran | oféndanse |

## 52. -ir verbs: Infinitive: vestirse    Present participle (gerund): vistiéndose    Past participle: vestido

vestirse (e → i), aburrirse, arrepentirse (e → ie), despedirse (e → i), desvestirse (e → i), dormirse(o → ue), herirse (e → ie), morirse (o → ue)

| PRESENT | PRETERITE | IMPERFECT | FUTURE | CONDITIONAL | PRESENT SUBJUNCTIVE | IMPERFECT SUBJUNCTIVE | IMPERATIVE |
|---|---|---|---|---|---|---|---|
| me visto | me vestí | me vestía | me vestiré | me vestiría | me vista | me vistiera | |
| te vistes | te vestiste | te vestías | te vestirás | te vestirías | te vistas | te vistieras | vístete /no te vistas |
| se viste | se vistió | se vestía | se vestirá | se vestiría | se vista | se vistiera | vístase (Ud.) |
| nos vestimos | nos vestimos | nos vestíamos | nos vestiremos | nos vestiríamos | nos vistamos | nos vistiéramos | vistámonos |
| os vestís | os vestisteis | os vestíais | os vestiréis | os vestiríais | os vistáis | os vistierais | vestíos /no os vistáis |
| se visten | se vistieron | se vestían | se vestirán | se vestirían | se vistan | se vistieran | vístanse |

*Index of Verbs*    **153**

# ABOUT THE AUTHORS

**Dr. Priscilla Gac-Artigas** teaches Spanish and French at Monmouth University, New Jersey, USA. She studied at the University of Puerto Rico, Middlebury College, the Sorbonne and the Department of Peninsular and Latin American Studies of the University of Franche-Comté, France.

In the pedagogical field she co-authored with Gustavo Gac-Artigas: **Sans Détour,** for French; **Directo al Grano,** for Spanish and **To the Point,** for English.

She is the editor of the Web site *Reflexiones: Essays on Contemporary Spanish-American Women Writers* (http:www.monmouth.edu/~pgacarti/index.html)

Dr. Gac-Artigas has been distinguished with the Elena Ralle-1994 Prize awarded by the University of Franche-Comté for "the research that best contributes to the knowledge and diffusion of Latin American culture."

She has completed her first novel: *Melina, conversaciones con el ser que serás.* (A Journal of Love)


**Gustavo Gac-Artigas,** Chilean writer and theater director, is author of *El solar de Ado, Tiempo de soñar, ¡E il orbo era rondo!, Dalibá la brujita del Caribe, Ex-Iliadas, Un asesinato corriente,* and *Seis historias Carrolltonesas.*

In theater: *El país de las lágrimas de sangre, Te llamamos Pablo-Pueblo, El huevo de Colón o Coca-Cola les ofrece un viaje de ensueños por América Latina, Cinco suspiros de eternidad,* and *Descubrimentando* (invented word created from descubriendo-experimentando).

Mr. Gac-Artigas has been distinguished with the Poetry Park Prize in the Netherlands, and as one of the Cecil and Ida Green Honors Professors by Texas Christian University, and has received critical acclaim for his writing.